A History of
CUMBERLAND
and WESTMORLAND

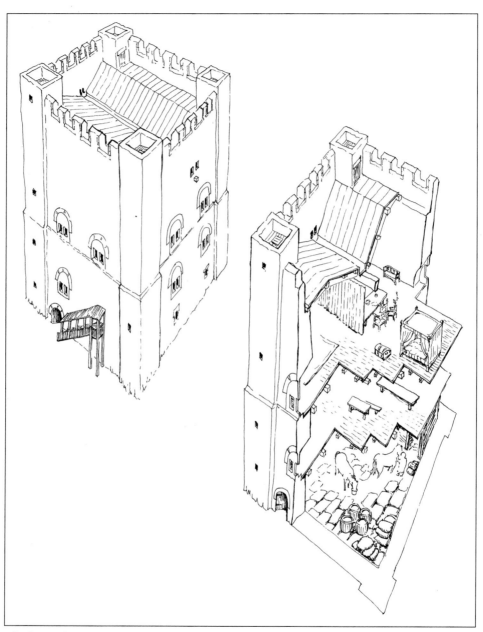

The keep of Appleby Castle as it probably appeared early in the 12th century. Redrawn from an illustration in Martin Holmes' book Appleby Castle *(1974) by kind permission of Ferguson Industrial Holdings Limited.*

THE DARWEN COUNTY
HISTORY SERIES

A History of
CUMBERLAND
and WESTMORLAND

William Rollinson

Drawings by David Kirk

Phillimore

First edition, 1978
Second edition, 1996

Published by
PHILLIMORE & CO. LTD.
Shopwyke Manor Barn, Chichester, West Sussex

ISBN 1 86077 009 6

Printed and bound in Great Britain by
BUTLER AND TANNER LTD.
London and Frome

Contents

List of Illustrations

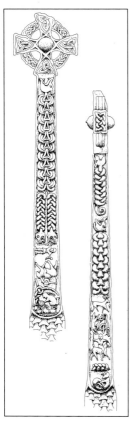

Gosforth Cross: west face (left) and south face (right).

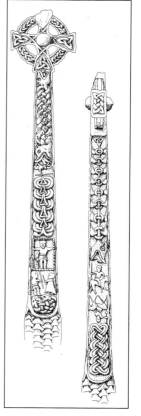

Gosforth Cross: east face (left) and north face (right).

List of Colour Illustrations

Acknowledgements

My thanks are due to the following for permission to reproduce photographs and documents: Megan Hadkins, II; Peter Fleming, 70; Jean Ward and Prof. Dennis Harding, 28; Prof. Barri Jones and Archaeological Surveys Ltd., Manchester, 15, 29; Bob Matthews, 23; Manchester Evening News, 138; the late Geoffrey Berry and the Friends of the Lake District, 142; the late Jane Smith, 135; Harry Fancy and the Whitehaven Museum and Heritage Centre, X, 117, 119; Cumbria County Council Sites and Monuments Record, 14; Cumbria Record Office, Carlisle, 88, 92; Cumbria Record Office, Barrow, 124; Andrew Lowe and the Lake District National Park Authority, 120; Barrow Public Library, 49, 115, 127, 128, 134; Sir John Clerk and the Scottish Record Office, 96; Lady Hothfield, 99. The National Trust kindly gave me permission to photograph the Taylor Longmire painting (XI).

The staff of Cumbria Record Office in Barrow, Kendal and Carlisle and Ron Smith in the Reference section of Barrow Library have dealt patiently with my many queries. I am grateful to Robert Hale Ltd. and the late Norman Nicholson for permission to quote from *Greater Lakeland* and to J.M. Dent who allowed me to reproduce maps from my *A History of Man in the Lake District.* Help and advice also came from Simon Crouch, Border Television plc, Dr. David Shotter and Dr. Paul Hindle, while the eagle eye of Christine Denmead saved me from many a typographical error. Alan Hodgkiss and the late Joan Treasure drew the maps with consummate skill and, finally, my sincere thanks go to David Kirk for the time, effort and enthusiasm he devoted to the line drawings. If any errors remain after all this assistance, the fault is entirely mine.

Photographs not acknowledged above were taken by the author.

WILLIAM ROLLINSON
Ulverston, January 1996

In memoriam:
Fred Barnes and Joe Bagley
Scholars, Gentlemen, Lancastrians—
and adopted Cumbrians

Preface

In 1974 the county of Cumbria was formed by an amalgamation of Cumberland, Westmorland, Lancashire North of the Sands, and a small piece of the West Riding of Yorkshire. The name adopted for the new county was not a 20th-century hybrid; it was, in fact, the name which the Celtic inhabitants gave to this region centuries ago—the land of the Cymry or compatriots. Yet for centuries before local government reorganisation recreated Cumbria, the area functioned as separate county units and the cartographers and administrators in Whitehall cannot entirely eradicate the independence and fierce pride of these old counties overnight; centuries of history cannot simply be changed for administrative convenience and there are many people who still regard themselves as Westmerians rather than Cumbrians; Furness folk continue to look across the shimmering sands of Morecambe Bay to Lancaster as they have done for centuries, rather than to distant Carlisle, the administrative centre of Cumbria. For the purposes of this book the former boundaries of Cumberland and Westmorland will be retained, and those who wish to learn more of Furness and Cartmel will find these areas considered in the companion volume to this, *A History of Lancashire* (Phillimore, 1976), written by my friend and colleague, the late J.J. Bagley.

Anyone writing a history of Cumberland and Westmorland will surely be aware of the great debt owed not only to the Cumberland and Westmorland Antiquarian and Archaeological Society, but also to historians such as R.S. Ferguson and Professor F. Haverfield in the 19th century, and Professors W.G. and R.G. Collingwood, Canon C.M.L. Bouch, Professor G.P. Jones, Miss C.I. Fell and Dr. J.D. Marshall in the 20th century. Historical geographers have also added to our knowledge of the landscape of Cumberland and Westmorland; Dr. Alan Harris's papers on industrial developments in the 19th century are enlightening, Dr. Angus Winchester's study of medieval Cumbria breaks new ground, and Dr. Paul Hindle's work on roads and communications is stimulating, while Dr. Roy Millward and Dr. Adrian Robinson have introduced a wider audience to the history of the landscape. To all these people, and to many who are here unnamed, I owe my thanks for, in the words of the great Cheshire cartographer, John Speed, 'I have put my sickle in other men's corne'.

WILLIAM ROLLINSON

1

The Prehistoric Period

The view from Scafell Pike on a clear day has thrilled and delighted countless fell walkers for generations; here, on the roof of England, a vast panorama of Cumberland and Westmorland is unrolled to delight the eye and uplift the spirit. In the east the great bulk of Bowfell with Windermere and the Pennines in the distance, in the south and south east, the Coniston and Furness Fells, and the rounded bastion of Black Combe jutting into the Irish Sea. To the west, deceptively looking as though they were a mere stone's throw away, the crags of Scafell seem to overshadow Wastwater, while away on the coastal plain the sinister chimneys of Sellafield point to where the milky-blue whale-back mass of the Isle of Man breaks the line of the horizon. North-westwards over the summit of Kirk Fell glints the Solway Firth with the hills of south-west Scotland in the distance, and northwards at the base of Great Gable, Borrowdale snakes towards Derwentwater and Skiddaw, while away to the north-east and east the Westmorland fells, High Street, Thornthwaite Crag, and the Langdale Pikes complete the circle. The summit of Scafell Pike is one of the most frequented peaks in the Lake District, yet thousands of pilgrims to this spot make the common, though mistaken, assumption that the scene which they behold is a 'natural' environment, a timeless and unchanging landscape which is fundamentally the same today as that witnessed by our Neolithic ancestors some five thousand years ago. Nothing could be further from the truth, for the present landscape is largely a man-made environment, the result of the interaction of man and his animals with the original vegetation pattern over a period of about 7,000 years.

The landscape which emerged from the waning ice sheets which once covered the Cumbrian dome was not unlike parts of Arctic Scandinavia today—a wilderness of ice-scoured rock and barren morainic debris. Gradually, however, hardy plant species began to colonise the desert; lichens, mosses and grasses, and shrubs such as juniper and the dwarf willow made their appearance. Subsequently, scattered pine and birch established themselves in the yet-developing soils, and ultimately the birch became dominant, followed from about 7000 B.C. onwards by hazel and, later, oak and elm. From 5500 B.C. onwards the natural vegetation cover of the north-west seems to have been fully established, and from our vantage point at the summit of Scafell Pike it would have been possible to see mixed oak forest swamping the lower fells and giving way to pine and birch woodland to a height of approximately two thousand feet, so that only the higher Lakeland fells were clear of the forest cover. This, then, was the natural climax vegetation which, if left unhindered by the interference of man and his animals, would probably be the same today; but this was not to be, for at some date yet undetermined, man, the principal actor, appeared on the stage.

Until recently it was assumed that during the final stages of the last ice age, when valley-head glaciers still occupied the corries of the Cumbrian mountains, the hostile and uncompromising environment so recently emerged from the ice precluded the existence of man. Within the last few years, however, archaeological work by C.R. Salisbury and others in Cartmel and Low Furness has raised the possibility that, some 10,000 years ago in certain climatically-favoured pockets around the shores of Morecambe Bay, Palaeolithic or Old Stone Age hunters may have followed their prey almost to the edge of the ice. By about 5500 B.C., however, the climate had ameliorated somewhat and it is to this Middle Stone Age, or Mesolithic period, we must look for the first clear signs of prehistoric man. Slight though it is, the evidence of tiny chipped flints, known as microliths, is significant, for these flakes are characteristic of these early Cumbrians. Possessing no knowledge of metals, primitive hunters and collectors depended for their very existence on flint, scavenged from the beaches of West Cumberland. Although small in size, these nodules of flint, originating from the glacial boulder clays, furnished prehistoric man with an efficient cutting edge, one which could cut through sinew and flesh, and, if properly worked, would scrape skins and fashion bone harpoons. Moreover, the sand-dune areas of the Cumbrian coasts were never densely forested and therefore offered certain advantages to a people not yet technically equipped to make inroads into the virgin forest which blanketed the fells. Finally, the proximity of the sea provided an additional source of food in the form of molluscs, fish and wild fowl, all valuable assets in the fight for survival. Not surprisingly, then, our Mesolithic ancestors chose littoral habitation sites and evidence from such areas as Eskmeals, Drigg, and St Bees in Cumberland substantiate this hypothesis. Furthermore, it seems that these Mesolithic people were almost entirely at the mercy of the environment for, with such limited technology, they were incapable of modifying or controlling it. However, pollen analysis has indicated that in the Ehenside area, near Beckermet, the vegetation cover at about 4000 B.C. was modified, perhaps as a result of primitive man burning areas of forest around his camps. If this is the case, then we have here one of the earliest episodes in the continuing story of the interaction of man and the environment.

On the whole, however, Middle Stone Age man made little impact on his environment, and it was left to his New Stone Age successors to implement the Neolithic Revolution. Arguably more dramatic and far-reaching than either the Agricultural or Industrial Revolutions of the 18th and 19th centuries, the Neolithic Revolution heralded a change in the economic well-being of prehistoric Cumbrians; as well as introducing the domestic arts of spinning, weaving and the making of pottery, these New Stone Age men were the first farmers and herders and evidence of their agricultural activities is found on the lighter, drier soils of the limestones, the sandstones, and the glacial sands and gravels which ring the Lake District fells.

Within the last 50 years, scientific techniques such as pollen analysis and radio-carbon dating have made possible the reconstruction of former environments with a degree of accuracy which would have amazed early researchers in this field. It is now known that during the centuries around 3000 B.C. the dramatic decline in elm pollen was a direct result of man's interference with the natural vegetation pattern, for it is believed that stock was fed on the highly nutritive leaves from this tree. With the accelerated forest clearances came a corresponding increase of grass and herb pollen together with the most significant of all weeds of cultivation, the plantain. In a number of instances, notably at Ehenside Tarn, near Beckermet, and Barfield Tarn, near Bootle, cereal pollen trapped in peat samples indicates that during the early part of the third millennium B.C. the first cultivators were active during the warm, dry sub-boreal climatic period. Yet it would be wrong to suggest that, with the advent of agriculture, New Stone Age man abandoned the hunting and collecting activities of his ancestors, for along the Cumberland coast in sand-dune sites such as Drigg, Low Ehenside and Eskmeals, hearths and kitchen middens display the same collection of sea-shells, fish-bones, small game and red deer bones, and flaked flints which are common in Middle Stone Age sites; only the presence of coarse, poorly-baked pottery indicates that these encampments belong to the Neolithic period.

Quite clearly a cultural revolution of the magnitude of the Neolithic Revolution could not have been achieved without significant technological advances. Foremost among these developments was the technique of grinding and polishing stone axes for this was the tool which wrought the revolution; described by Professor J.G.D. Clark as a response to an ecological situation, the polished stone axe was a more effective implement than the flint hand axe. Moreover, the polished stone axe was more than a mere response to the challenge of the forest; it was, when hafted as a hoe or mattock, one of the first agricultural tools. Although roughed-out and polished stone axes have been found in the Lake counties for centuries, the major source of these tools was not discovered until 1947

1 Both axes are made from the fine-grained volcanic rock found in the central fells of the Lake District. That on the left has been roughed out prior to finishing; that on the right has been finely polished and is ready for hafting. With tools such as these, Neolithic Cumbrians could clear small areas in dense forest in order to grow crops and rear animals.

INCHES

2   In this experiment, a faulted Langdale rough-out stone axe was polished some 4,500 years after it was first made, hafted in an ash handle and used to fell a birch tree. The tree was felled in just over 20 minutes.

when a chance find revealed the important workings on the screes below Pike of Stickle in Great Langdale. Subsequently other factory sites were discovered on nearby Harrison Stickle, Glaramara, and near to the summit of Scafell Pike. It is clear that the major factor influencing the location of this industry—for it was nothing less—was the presence of the fine-grained volcanic ash, part of the Borrowdale Volcanic series that forms the central fells of the Lake District. Indeed, it might be suggested that as well as being the first farmers, these Neolithic Cumbrians were the first field geologists, actively seeking out and exploiting that volcanic rock which, like flint, chipped conchoidally and produced a sharp yet durable cutting edge.

Following the roughing-out of the stone axes at a height of over 1,800 feet above sea level—a process, which, incidentally, involved the rejection of faulty specimens by a primitive quality-control system— they were then taken to the various habitation sites for polishing with sharp quartz sand and sandstone grinders. Later the finished axes were bartered and some found their way to the Isle of Man, south-west Scotland, and Lothians, Yorkshire, and the chalklands of southern England, indicating that axes from Cumberland and Westmorland were a much-prized commodity. Radio-carbon dates for a site at Thunacar Knott, almost on the Cumberland-Westmorland boundary above Great Langdale, suggest that the factory was active around the period 2730 and 2550 B.C., but it seems probable that these sites continued to supply local needs well into the Bronze Age, reflecting the natural conservatism of this north-west area.

All the evidence which has so far come to light appears to suggest that the manufacture of roughed-out axes within the high fells was a seasonal activity, probably occupying the summer months. By an extension of this hypothesis, it might equally well be agreed that the axes were polished at sites along the coast during the winter. Although in other parts of Britain, rectangular wooden dwellings were in use during the New Stone Age, none has yet been traced within Cumberland and Westmorland, but at Ehenside Tarn one of the most rewarding Neolithic settlement sites was investigated in the early 1870s when the shallow tarn was drained for agricultural purposes. A number of ancient hearths revealed during the drainage operation yielded up a remarkable range of wooden and stone implements which reflect the economic livelihood of these early West Cumbrians; as well as a variety of polished and partly polished stone axes, including one still in its wooden haft, fragments of decorated coarse and fine pottery, sandstone polishing tools, a saucer quern for the grinding of grain, and

I   *Pike of Stickle, Great Langdale, Westmorland. Five thousand years ago, this fellside was the scene of one of the first craft industries in Britain—the roughing out of stone axes which were then transported to the coast for polishing. The stone axe factory was first located in 1947.*

II   *The Castlerigg stone circle, near Keswick, Cumberland. Certainly one of the most dramatic elements in the cultural landscape, these massive stones were probably placed here early in the late Neolithic or early Bronze Age, perhaps for ceremonial purposes.*

III *Hardknott Roman fort, Eskdale, Cumberland. Perched high above Eskdale, and overshadowed by the Scafell range, this 'enchanted fortress in the air' once commanded the road between the forts at Ambleside and Ravenglass on the coast.*

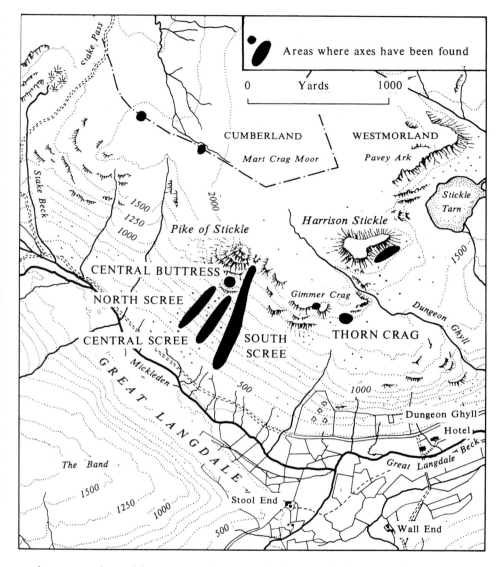

Areas where axes have been found

0   Yards   1000

CUMBERLAND   WESTMORLAND

Mart Crag Moor   Pavey Ark

Stickle Tarn

Harrison Stickle

Pike of Stickle

CENTRAL BUTTRESS

NORTH SCREE   Gimmer Crag

Dungeon Ghyll

CENTRAL SCREE   SOUTH SCREE   THORN CRAG

GREAT LANGDALE

Mickleden

Dungeon Ghyll Hotel

Great Langdale Beck

The Band

Stool End

Wall End

3 *The Great Langdale axe factory sites. Here prehistoric man roughed out stone axes which were then taken to the coast for polishing.*

various wooden objects were discovered. Most of these artefacts are now in the British Museum and radio-carbon tests on the wooden tools have suggested dates ranging from 3124 to 1570 B.C.

Early in the second millennium B.C. a group of prehistoric 'off-comers' arrived in Cumberland and Westmorland, probably by way of the Pennine passes from Yorkshire and Northumberland. Essentially herdsmen and hunters rather than agriculturalists, these newcomers, known to archaeologists as Beaker people, from the characteristic drinking vessel often buried with them, settled in the Eden valley and the Cumberland coastal plain. The significance of the Beaker people is that they were the vanguard of yet another revolution—the transformation from the Stone Age to the Bronze

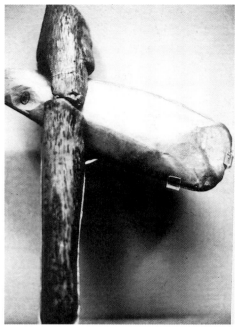

5 *Early Bronze-Age tanged and barbed flint arrowheads from Eskmeals, Cumberland.*

Age. It seems, too, that these new settlers were responsible in part for the construction of the great stone circles which continue to puzzle and enthral historians and scientists. Why were they built? No one can answer this question with certainty; perhaps they were intended for ceremonial purposes, but one can only guess at the rituals. The theory that the circles were giant astronomical clocks or prehistoric computers, fascinating though it is, has not found universal favour with pre-historians. One thing is certain, however; the engineering techniques required to move these large stones weighing several tons required a degree of social co-operation not previously apparent.

The best known of the Cumberland megalithic circles is undoubtedly at Castlerigg, east of Keswick; the circle, made up of 39 irregular-shaped boulders, is surrounded by some of the finest mountain scenery in the Lake District with Blencathra commanding the northern skyline and the great bulk of the Helvellyn range dominating the south-east. At Swinside in South Cumberland a similar ring of standing stones occupies a site on the bleak, windswept flanks of Black Combe overlooking the Duddon estuary, while at Shap in Westmorland six granite boulders are all that remain of a stone circle partly destroyed in the 19th century by railway construction.

Likewise, the great stone circle, Grey Yauds, some three miles south east of Cumwhitton in Cumberland, is now no more. Of all the megalithic circles in the two counties, the largest is Long Meg and her Daughters, near Little Salkeld. The circle of stones is over 100 yards in diameter and Long Meg herself is a 12-foot high monolith standing some 70 feet away. Although not strictly a large stone circle, the Mayburgh henge monument at Eamont Bridge is certainly a conspicuous feature on the landscape; formed of a massive circular embankment of stones rising in some places to over 15 feet high, it has a single entrance on the east and a large monolith near the centre, the only one of seven stones still standing in the 18th century. The date and purpose of this earthwork and the nearby King Arthur's Round Table cannot be determined, but they are, together with the megalithic circles, an integral part of man's signature on the landscape.

During the early and middle Bronze Age the climate was warmer and calmer than now and navigation between Ireland and England, Scotland and Wales was comparatively simple, even for open boats or currachs. Certainly the cultural connection between Ireland and Cumberland and Westmorland is apparent for there are striking similarities between many

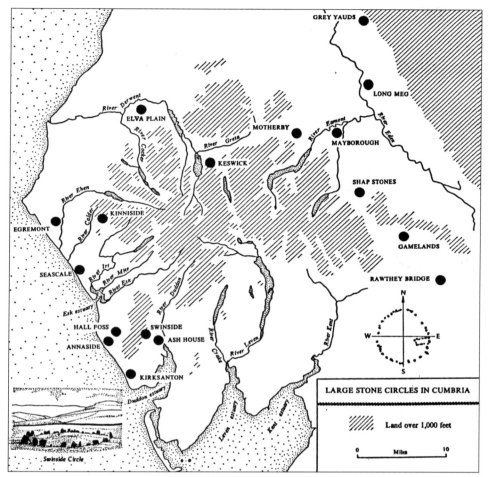

8 *Early Bronze-Age food vessel from Plumpton, near Penrith, Cumberland. Impressions of grain have been found in the clay of this pot. Height: approx. 6 inches.*

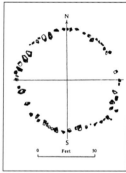

9 *Swinside stone circle, near Millom, South Cumberland.*

6 *Megalithic (large stone) circles in Cumbria. The north point on this map shows a plan of the Castlerigg Circle near Keswick.*

7 *Sheltering in the lee of Black Combe, the Swinside circle is one of the lesser-known megalithic monuments. Described by one authority as 'the loveliest of all the circles', it lies at a height of 700 feet above sea level and commands fine views across the Duddon estuary to the hills of Furness.*

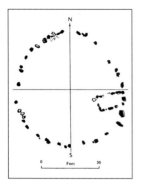

10 *Castlerigg stone circle, near Keswick, Cumberland.*

11 *Spiral and concentric circles on a stone forming part of the circle known as Little Meg, Maughanby, Cumberland.*

12 *Bronze-Age collared urn from Barnscar, Muncaster, Cumberland. Height: approx. 5 inches.*

of the bronze axes, spearheads, daggers and rapiers found in the two counties and those found on the other side of the Irish Sea. Some of these weapons undoubtedly originated in Ireland and were imported into Cumberland and Westmorland, while others were manufactured here but based on Irish prototypes. Further evidence for a possible Ireland-Cumbria connection is provided by a number of decorated stones engraved with concentric circles, spirals, and other designs. Best seen on burial circles at Little Meg, Maughanby, at Graysonlands, Glassonby, at Old Parks, Kirkoswald and on Long Meg herself, these decorations bear a remarkable likeness to the designs on the Neolithic Passage-Graves of the Boyne area, notably New Grange and Knowth, and it might be supposed that Bronze-Age traders, familiar with the Irish designs, inscribed similar patterns on the Cumbrian stones.

As well as the large stone circles, the numerous cairns and burial circles scattered throughout Cumberland and Westmorland are further evidence for the activity of Bronze-Age Man. Irresistibly attractive to 19th-century amateur archaeologists, many of these cairns have been destroyed and their contents scattered, but over 60 sites have been carefully excavated and proved to date from the Bronze Age, and many remain to be explored. In Cumberland the most important cairnfields occur in areas such as Ennerdale Forest, in the vicinity of Caldbeck and Hesket Newmarket, on Stockdale Moor, in the parish of Ponsonby, east of the river Calder, at Barnscar, west of Devoke Water, and on lonely Burnmoor above Eskdale. In Westmorland there is a concentration on Moor Divock, south east of Pooley Bridge, and also around Crosby Ravensworth, Crosby Garrett and Shap. Many of these cairns are located between 500 and 1,000 feet above sea level, suggesting that during the mild, drier weather of the early and middle Bronze Age a movement into the higher fells was initiated.

Towards the end of the Bronze Age, between 800 and 500 B.C., fluctuations in climate resulted in wetter, stormier conditions, which inevitably made contact with Ireland more hazardous. At the same time, increasing environmental difficulties probably meant that some of the higher, exposed settlements were abandoned in favour of more sheltered and hospitable sites. Exactly when iron-using Celtic people arrived in Cumberland and Westmorland remains an open question, but it seems probable that in the second or third century B.C. they arrived in the Eden Valley and the eastern valleys of the Lake District, having crossed the Pennines from Yorkshire. Technically more sophisticated than their Bronze-Age neighbours, they introduced an advanced mixed farming economy, in which horses were bred for riding and as draught animals, and a degree of craftsmanship in metal hitherto unknown.

Research in Northumberland has suggested that early pre-Roman Iron-Age huts were circular, wooden constructions and that during the Roman occupation these huts and enclosures were built in stone; by analogy it might be supposed that a similar situation applied in Cumberland and Westmorland. Certainly there are many examples of the stone-walled enclosures containing circular stone-built huts within the two counties; the best known is Ewe Close, near Crosby Ravensworth, but others are still being discovered. Within the last three decades aerial photography has shown that the Cumberland plain between the Solway and the Lake District uplands and the Eden valley were colonised by Iron-Age groups. At Wolsty Hall, Silloth, aerial photographs revealed an oval pallisaded enclosure surrounding a circular wooden hut, and at Risehow, near Maryport, the unmistakable outline of a cattle enclosure was observed, while at Crosshill, near Penrith, Professor Barri Jones has excavated a Romano-British settlement first dis-

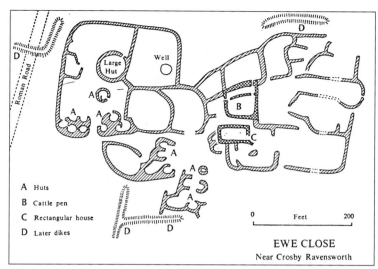

A Huts
B Cattle pen
C Rectangular house
D Later dikes

0   Feet   200

EWE CLOSE
Near Crosby Ravensworth

covered from the air. Nothing is visible on the surface of any of these constructions; only their ghostly shadows, viewed from the air, betray their former existence, yet these outlines conform to the pattern of pre-Roman Iron-Age farms in the south of England. The application of aerial photography has certainly added much to our knowledge of settlement in Northern Cumberland and Westmorland and within the last three decades many habitation sites have been located where only a few were previously known.

Although the period of the late Iron Age was one of political disturbance, the hill-forts in Cumberland and Westmorland are few in number

13 *Ewe Close is one of the largest and best known Romano-British settlements in the north of England. The huts and animal pens are clearly discernible and east of the settlement there are distinct remains of stone-fenced 'Celtic' fields. The Roman road ran close to the fort in order that the troops could keep a watchful eye on the inhabitants.*

14 *Aughertree Fell prehistoric farmstead, Cumberland. Here a droveway clearly leads from the unenclosed grazing to an oval, enclosed farmstead. Such enclosures have recently been termed 'banjo farmsteads' and it is likely that they date from the Iron Age.*

15 *Kirkbampton, Cumberland. This aerial photograph shows a roughly circular enclosure and the darker patches indicate the position of huts within the enclosure. The settlement probably dates from the Romano-British period. There are no surface remains to be seen, but from the air the differential growth of cereal crops makes identification easy. Within the last thirty years more than 170 of these sites have been located where only a few were previously known.*

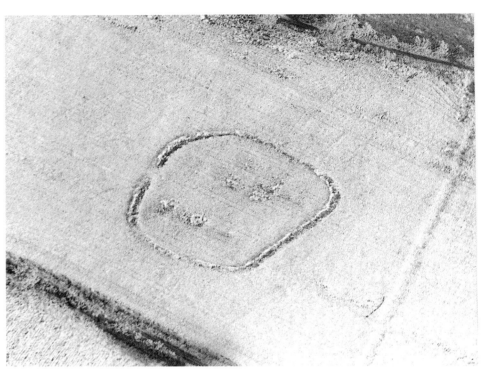

16 *Bronze bridle bit from Place Fell, Ullswater, late 1st century A.D.*

and small in size when measured against the great fort which crowns the summit of Ingleborough in neighbouring Yorkshire. The most impressive is that on Carrock Fell, a spur of the Caldbeck fells, dominating Mungrisdale at a height of 2,175 feet above sea level. Professor R.G. Collingwood argued convincingly that this fort might have been the local headquarters of the Brigantian tribe which occupied this part of Cumberland and he further extends his hypothesis by supposing that in the first century A.D. the Romans slighted the ramparts so that it would not constitute a threat to Roman authority. The other forts are insignificant in comparison; Castlesteads, at Natland near Kendal, and Croglam Castle near Kirkby Stephen are small, while Castle Crag, high above the Jaws of Borrowdale, and the other Castle Crag overlooking Haweswater both have dramatic sites, but their history remains to be unravelled.

2

The Romans in Cumberland and Westmorland

Referring to the far north-west of England, Professor R.G. Collingwood once remarked that 'we are almost at vanishing point in the scale of Romanisation', and of course he was correct in that there is little trace in Cumbrian dialect or place-names of over three centuries of Roman rule. Moreover, the antiquarian and historian will look in vain for evidence of

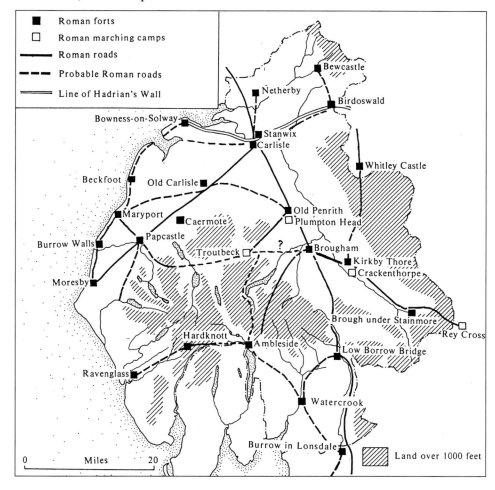

17 *Roman forts in Cumberland and Westmorland.*

18 *The Hermes Stone, Brough. Discovered during the restoration of the church in 1879, the stone commemorates the death of Hermes of Commagene in Syria. He was in his 16th year when he died. Originally the inscription was thought to be runic but in 1884 it was proved to be written in Greek. It reads: 'Hermes of Commagene here, Young Hermes, in his sixteenth year Entombed by fate, before his day, Beholding, let the traveller say: "Fair youth, my greeting to thy shrine, Though but a mortal course be thine Since all too soon thou wings't thy flight From realms of speech to realms of night, Yet no misnomer art thou shown Who with thy namesake god art flown".'*

the villas, imperial buildings, markets, and industries which were common in southern Britain during Roman times, for Cumbria formed part of the Military Zone, the largely upland area of the country in which the introduction of Roman civilisation came a poor second to the subjugation of the often troublesome Brigantes. Yet within Cumberland and Westmorland the impact of Rome on the environment is still plain to see, emblazoned over the fells in the form of military installations, roads, forts, mile castles, bath-houses and that most dramatic and elaborate of all defensive systems, Hadrian's Wall, a monument to Rome's might and military genius.

The Roman legions entered this area sometime after A.D. 71, when Petillius Cerialis crushed the Brigantes and, although the exact sequence of events has not been determined, it seems that the first penetration came by way of Stainmore, where the great marching camp at Rey Cross on the main road from York probably marks the fortifications of the vanguard. From there, the route seems to have proceeded through Brough, along the east bank of the Eden to Kirkby Thore, Brougham, and so to Carlisle, a route traced out by two other marching camps at Crackenthorpe and Plumpton Head. Some years later, during Agricola's governorship (A.D. 77-84), this north-west territory was consolidated by the construction of a road west of the Pennines from Chester through the wild Lune gorge to the fort at Low Borrow Bridge and then on to Brougham where it joined the earlier road from York. By A.D. 79 these two roads had provided a framework on which further penetration could be based, and by the end of the first century other roads probably existed, notably the Stanegate linking Carlisle with Corbridge along which forts at Old Church, Brampton, and Nether Denton were dotted like beads on a string. Similarly, another first-century road struck south-westwards from Carlisle towards the Cumberland coast and on this forts at Old Carlisle (near Wigton), Caermote, and Papcastle, near Cockermouth, were strategically located.

Possibly the roads which can be traced intermittently from Papcastle over the Whinlatter Pass towards Keswick and from Old Penrith towards the Cumberland Troutbeck were also engineered during the first century. At Troutbeck are the remains of three temporary encampments first identified by that assiduous 18th-century guide-book writer, Father Thomas

West, but rediscovered on aerial photographs taken by Dr. St. Joseph. If, as Thomas West argued, the roads converged on Keswick, then it seemed to him logical to suppose that a Roman fort had been located somewhere in the vicinity. So far nothing has yet been found, but careful surveillance may yet vindicate the scholarly Jesuit priest.

The long-held belief that many of Lakeland's Roman forts were established by Agricola in the period between A.D. 79 and 84 has not withstood recent examination. Excavations undertaken by Dr. T.W. Potter at Watercrook, south of Kendal, have shown that this fort, once thought to be one of the earliest of the Agricola fortifications, could not have been established here before A.D. 90, and it now seems likely that Roman troops pressed on to the Carlisle area and the north Cumberland plain before turning their attention to the fells and dales of central Cumbria. Having pacified the Eden Valley, the suppression of the troublesome hill tribes was accompanied by the simple but effective expedient of a road running from Watercrook to the head of Windermere and then westward through the fells to Eskdale and the sea at Ravenglass. Although not the most spectacular of the Lakeland forts, Watercrook, in the valley of the Kent, is far from uninteresting and recent excavations have produced evidence of an early timber fort on this site, which was rebuilt in stone in the late Hadrianic or early Antonine period. Finds of early 4th-century pottery indicate the possibility of occupation at this time, though not necessarily by troops.

19 *A Roman monumental stone found near Murrill Hill, Carlisle.*

It is believed that from Watercrook two roads ran northwards; one in a north-easterly direction to link with the main Lune Valley route at Low Borrow Bridge, the other in a north-westerly direction to Galava, the fort at the head of Windermere. Here in Borrans Field, with summer holiday-makers picnicking in the park, and steamers arriving and departing from Waterhead pier, it is difficult to imagine the Roman fort set on the marshy delta of the rivers Rothay and Brathay and surrounded by densely wooded fells; indeed, it is easy to overlook the fences which mark the excavated remains of the fort, for this is not one of Lakeland's great tourist attractions, but, for those who know its history, this is a fascinating place. Excavations conducted by Professor R.G. Collingwood between 1913 and 1920 revealed two forts on the same site, the older being a turf and timber fort which was later covered by an artificially-constructed platform on which the stone-built fort of the second century was located, safely above flood level. In the centre of the fort stood the three main buildings, the granary, the Principia or headquarters, and the Commandant's house. Built of local stone, heavily buttressed and with a slate roof, the granary was one of the most stoutly-constructed buildings within the fort. Its floors were supported on long, low parallel walls in order to allow air to circulate and to discourage vermin. The Principia, arranged around a courtyard, contained the chapel in which the legionary standards were kept, and below that was an underground strong room reached by a short flight of stone steps which can still be seen. The barrack blocks, probably constructed of timber, have left no trace on the landscape and it is highly likely that they

20 *The turf and stone forts at Galava, near Ambleside, Westmorland. The first fort built on this site, marked A on this plan, was liable to flooding and so was abandoned. The second fort, marked B, was built of stone and was constructed on an artificial platform which covered the site of the original turf-built fort.*

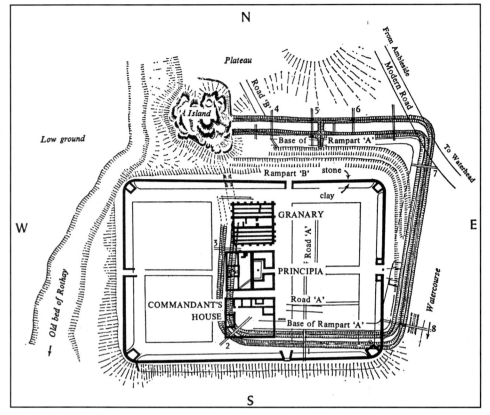

21 *The granary at Ambleside Roman Fort contained sufficient grain to support a cohort of 500 men for a year. For security reasons, it was built entirely of stone, and with a slate roof. The remains of the buttresses may be seen on the left of this photograph and the floor was laid over the low, parallel foundations to allow air to circulate and to discourage vermin.*

22 *The second Roman fort at Ambleside. W.G. Collingwood drew this reconstruction of the second fort at Galava. The stone walls and foundations may still be observed in Borrans field and the three main buildings, from left to right, the Commandant's House, the Principia or H.Q., and the granaries, can be identified.*

were destroyed by fire for it seems that the fort was attacked by hostile tribes on several occasions. Despite this, however, a small *vicus* or civil settlement grew up outside the walls of the fort and here leather working and other crafts were carried out; it was here, too, that in 1963 a stark and dramatic reminder of hostilities was uncovered—a gravestone bearing the inscription:

> TO THE GOOD GODS OF THE
> UNDERWORLD
> FLAVIUS FUSCINUS RETIRED
> FROM THE CENTURIONSHIP
> LIVED 55 YEARS
>
> TO THE GOOD GODS OF THE
> UNDERWORLD
> FLAVIUS ROMANUS, RECORD
> CLERK,
> LIVED FOR 35 YEARS
> KILLED IN THE FORT BY THE
> ENEMY.

23 *Perhaps the most dramatic Roman discovery ever made in Westmorland, this crudely-carved tombstone from the fort at Galava, near Ambleside, marked the grave of a retired centurion, Flavius Fuscinus, and a records clerk, Flavius Romanus, who was 'killed in the fort by the enemy'.*

Exactly when the cohort of 500 auxiliary troops evacuated Galava is uncertain; evidence from pottery and coins suggests an occupation even in the second half of the 4th century and it might be supposed that the fort remained manned until the final withdrawal from the Wall after A.D. 383. And perhaps five centuries later a group of newcomers encountered the overgrown ruin and called it, in their own language, 'Borrans' which is a Norse word meaning 'a heap of stones'.

Recent research and excavation has suggested that a Roman road ran north from Galava, over Kirkstone Pass, where a clear man-made terraceway can be detected to the west of the present road, on via Ullswater and Matterdale to join the road from Troutbeck (Cumberland) to Old Penrith near Whitbarrow Hall. Similarly, from Galava a road may have branched north-eastward along Stock Gill to meet the road over the High Street range in the vicinity of Troutbeck (Westmorland), but so far research has failed to identify such a route. On the flanks of Froswick above the cultivation level and on High Street itself, the Roman road can readily be identified, particularly after a light fall of snow, and it can be followed by stoutly-shod fellwalkers to the vicinity of Tirril, two miles south of Penrith, where it is lost in the cultivated fields of the Eamont Valley, though its objective was clearly Brougham on the main Ribchester-Carlisle road. Rising to a height of over 2,000 feet this is surely one of the most exciting of the Roman roads in the north, yet the reason for its construction remains unclear; certainly it cannot have been strategically important for the steep slopes, particularly in the Troutbeck area, would have restricted the use of

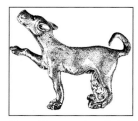

24 *A bronze dog, 2˝ ins. long. This Roman statuette from Kirkby Thore, Westmorland, has been described as a masterpiece of second-century naturalistic art.*

wheeled vehicles, yet, for all that, the road seems to have been in use during the period after the Roman withdrawal, and its 13th-century name, Brettestrete, the street or road of the Britons, perhaps indicates its antiquity.

Exciting though the High Street road certainly is, the road which struck into the fells westward from Galava is undoubtedly its equal. Although indistinct in the valley of the Brathay, from Fell Foot in Little Langdale to Brotherilkeld Farm in Eskdale the road runs for the most part in wild, uncultivated terrain, and can therefore be fairly readily identified as it clings to the fellside contours, switchbacks over Wrynose Pass to Duddon and zig-zags its way over Hardknott Pass to Hardknott Fort perched eyrie-like on a shoulder of the fell 800 feet above sea level. Hardknott 'Castle' is surely one of the most remarkable Roman forts in Britain; the views from its walls are breathtaking—south-westwards down Eskdale to the sea and the Isle of Man beyond, northwards to the awesome Scafell range, and southwards to the rocky pyramid of Harter Fell, but its strategic location is equally striking. To the north and west the crags of Bell Stand fall sharply almost to the valley floor, while to the south the fort is bounded by the deep valley of Hardknott Gill, making attack from these directions virtually impossible; only on the north-east side was the fort vulnerable, a factor appreciated by the Roman military engineers, for on this side they excavated deep trenches in the solid bedrock.

Within the walls of the fort the carefully preserved remains of the three main buildings, the granary, the administration block, and the apparently unfinished commander's house, may be seen, similar in plan to those at Galava, Ambleside. Mediobogdum, the probable Roman name for Hardknott Fort, can scarcely have been the most popular posting in the Roman army for, as well as the rigours of life in a bleak fell-side barrack block, the fort lacked the facilities offered by a *vicus* or civil settlement. However, perhaps after a hard day's drilling on the parade ground above

25 *'... that lone Camp on Hardknott's height, Whose Guardians bent the knee to Jove and Mars ...' (Wordsworth). Hardknott Fort housed a cohort of 500 auxiliary troops and, according to a stone found in 1964, was built 'for the Emperor Caesar Trajan Hadrian Augustus' by the Fourth Cohort of the Dalmatians, troops recruited from the Adriatic province of Dalmatia in former Yugoslavia. This photograph shows the remains of the* principia *or headquarters building, with the remains of the commandant's residence in the background.*

the fort, the auxiliary troops found warmth and comfort in the bath house, no doubt playing dice and gambling away their pay. The bath house is a simple three-roomed building on the fellside below the south-east gateway of the fort; it incorporated a cold room *(frigidarium)*, a warm room *(tepidarium)*, and a hot room *(caldarium)* heated by a small furnace. In addition, a

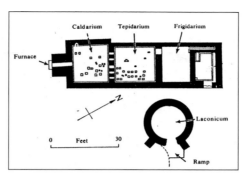

26 *The bath-house, Hardknott Roman Fort*

circular beehive-shaped building nearby housed the *laconicum*, a hot, sauna-type bath, heated by its own furnace. Water for the baths was supplied by a small fell-side stream known today as Campsike.

The dramatic discovery in 1964 of an inscribed stone near to the south-east gate records that the fort was erected 'for the Emperor Caesar Trajan Hadrian Augustus' by the Fourth Cohort of Dalmatians, troops recruited from the Adriatic province of Dalmatia, in former Yugoslavia. Finds of pottery and coins suggest that the fort was occupied during the period A.D. 120-138 and again between A.D. 160 to 197, after which it seems to have been abandoned. What fate befell Mediobogdum can only be surmised; Professor R.G. Collingwood was convinced that the vacated fort was left in the hands of a caretaker and that the bath-house was converted into an inn where travellers along the Roman road might find refreshment and accommodation.

For all its fine views of Eskdale and the surrounding mountains, the time to see Hardknott Fort is on a still, misty day, when the only sounds are those of the croak of the ravens and the muffled roar of Hardknott Gill and the only visitors are Herdwick sheep cropping the green turf. It then requires but little imagination to picture the crenellated battlements and the huge, iron-studded south-east gateway standing open to admit a straining, creaking ox-cart into the fort, while away on the parade ground the strident note of a brass horn, the clash of metal against metal, and the strange, outlandish voices can all be clearly heard. Such is the romance of Hardknott.

From Hardknott Fort the Roman road can be traced a short way down the fellside, but is soon lost in a small plantation and later in agricultural land on the floor of the Esk Valley. Nevertheless, there can be little doubt that its destination was Glannaventa, 'the town on the bank', perhaps a reflection of the location of the fort and its adjoining civil settlement on a bluff overlooking

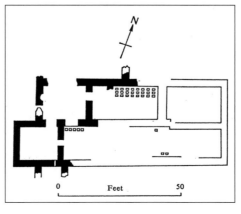

27 *Roman bath-house, Walls Castle, Ravenglass, Cumberland.*

28 *The Roman fort at Old Carlisle, near Wigton, Cumberland, was one of the main strongpoints on the road which ran south-westwards from Carlisle to Papcastle, near Cockermouth, and Moresby on the coast. The low sunlight clearly picks out the ditches, embankments and gates of the fort as well as a well-defined civil settlement along the road leading out of the fort (centre, top).*

the confluence of the rivers Mite and Esk. It seems that Glannaventa had certain port functions and it might be supposed that forts in the area were supplied by sea through Ravenglass, but it is also possible that the fort was part of the flanking defences of Hadrian's Wall. Although nothing remains of the fort itself, the bath house, known locally as Walls Castle, is an outstanding structure, for, according to Professor R.G. Collingwood, it is the best-preserved Roman building in the north of England. Built of the local sandstone, the bath house still stands to the full height of its walls, 12 feet; indeed, many visitors pass by the building taking it to be nothing more than the ruin of an 18th-century cottage.

From Glannaventa a Roman road may have run northwards to forts at Moresby, Burrow Walls, Maryport, and Beckfoot, and it now seems certain that these four cohort forts were built as part of the Hadrianic defences of the western end of the great wall which bears his name. Perhaps it was from one of these West Cumberland forts that towards the close of the 4th century the son of a high-born Roman was kidnapped by sea raiders and taken to Ireland. His name was Patrick, and subsequently he was to write his name indelibly in the annals of Dark-Age Britain. Mr. R.L. Bellhouse's remarkable field-work has uncovered many of the mile fortlets and watchtowers which existed between the forts, proving conclusively that the system of fort, milecastle, and watchtower was simply an extension of the wall fortifications. More recently, Professor Barri Jones has investigated in the Silloth area marks first seen on aerial photographs and has concluded that the fortifications south of Bowness-on-Solway were linked not only with a system of roads, ditches and embankments, but also by a form of wooden palisade, a feature previously known only on the Rhine frontier.

Of all the Roman remains in Cumberland, none can compete in magnitude and interest with Hadrian's Wall, and rightly so, for this is the best-preserved frontier barrier in the whole of the Roman Empire, stretching for 73 English miles from Wallsend on the river Tyne to Bowness-on-Solway. The western end of the wall from the river Irthing to the Solway coast was at first built of turf, there being no lime in that area; mile castles in this section were built of turf and timber and only the turrets were of stone. Although the construction of the turf wall commenced in A.D. 122, just like its stone-built equivalent east of the Irthing, by A.D. 138 rebuilding in stone had been started, but the total conversion was not completed until A.D. 163. According to his biographer, 'Hadrian constructed the wall to separate the Romans from the barbarians', and, as well as the wall itself, the fortifications involved the building of six forts at regular intervals along the Cumberland section of the wall at Birdoswald, Castlesteads, Stanwix (Carlisle), Burgh-de-Sands, Drumburgh and Bowness-on-Solway. In addition, south of the wall, the vallum, a flat-bottomed ditch with an earth embankment on either side, was constructed in order to demarcate a militarised frontier zone into which unauthorised people from the province were not admitted. With the construction of the wall the earlier frontier forts at such places as Old Church, Brampton and Nether Denton were made obsolete.

The fort at Birdoswald is the best preserved of all the Cumberland wall forts, though a farmhouse obscures the north-western corner. Certainly the fort has a fine site overlooking the deep gorge of the Irthing valley; indeed, one 19th-century Earl of Carlisle expressed the opinion that the view across the valley was the finest in Cumberland and compared it with the view at Troy! Today a splendid visitor centre occupies part of the site where once stood the

29 *Hadrian's Wall. This aerial photograph shows the junction of the Turf and Stone wall west of Birdoswald, Cumberland. Originally the Wall was built of turf in this area and replaced later by the Stone Wall. West of Birdoswald, however, the two lines were divergent; here the course of the Turf Wall, backed by the vallum, may be seen slightly to the right of centre, while the course of the Stone Wall, identified by its ditch and the road along its top, can be picked out to the left.*

30 *A Roman shoe from Birdoswald, Cumberland.*

31 *Female pottery mask on the neck of a third-century Roman jug from Burgh by Sands, Cumberland.*

granaries and headquarters building, but who can stand on the wall at Birdoswald on a wild March day when the scudding clouds throw a pattern of light and shade over the great frontier as it snakes eastwards over the fells, and not thrill to the knowledge that they stand on the very boundary of the Roman Empire? At Castlesteads, seven miles west of Birdoswald, and again at Stanwix, a suburb of Carlisle, little remains to be seen of the Roman forts, though the latter housed a cavalry unit of almost 1,000 men, substantiating the claim that Carlisle was the command centre of the wall system. West of Carlisle the Wall enters the less dramatic countryside of the Solway plain; the forts here have left little trace on the landscape, either being completely built over or else robbed for their freestone in the 16th and 17th centuries.

The history of the Wall is one of evacuations and re-fortifications; in A.D. 139 Roman forces advanced into Scotland and the Antonine Wall was built between the Forth and the Clyde and Hadrian's Wall was left in the care of a token force. Between A.D. 158 and 184 the Antonine Wall was abandoned and Hadrian's Wall once again became the frontier of the Roman Empire until A.D. 197 when the Governor of Britain, Clodius Albinus, took away most of the garrison to support him in his unsuccessful fight for the throne and the Wall was over-thrown. History repeated itself almost exactly a century later when the frontier was breached a second time when the usurper Allectus rallied the garrison behind him. The Wall was rebuilt by Constantius Chlorus about A.D. 300, but once again over-thrown in 367 when Britain was invaded by the 'barbarian conspiracy' of the Picts, the Scots, and the Saxons. Hastily repaired by Count Theodosius, it remained but a shadow of its former self; the *vici* were evacuated and the forts ceased to be occupied at the close of the fourth century. It should be remembered, however, that during the prolonged periods of peace the Wall had an important political and economic function; an aerial survey of territories north and south of the Wall has shown that settlement was considerably more pronounced south of the Wall than north of it, an eloquent testimony to 'the Roman Peace'.

The end of Roman rule came not with a bang but a whimper; in A.D. 410 the Emperor Honorius signed one of the most dramatic documents in history—it was a reply to a British request for aid against the barbarians, but Rome was powerless to act and Honorius had to tell the Britons to look after themselves. With this, the Dark Ages begin, peopled with shadowy, half-perceived figures like Arthur, Vortigern and Urien, part myth, part reality. For some time Romanised Britons lingered on, firm in their belief that they were heirs to Roman civilisation; at Carlisle it seems that the trappings of Roman urban life remained until the seventh century, for in A.D. 685 St Cuthbert was shown the town walls and a fountain, suggesting that the Roman aqueducts still functioned. Elsewhere, however, the veneer of Romanisation crumbled under the attacks from the Picts and the Scots, and the forts on the Wall may have become refuges for brigands and horse thieves. By the end of the 6th century the old Celtic traditions and language had re-asserted themselves and the Roman Interlude was over.

3

The Men of the North

Arguably the most fascinating period in the history of the north-west, the Dark Ages between the fifth and the eighth centuries, still retain their enigma; the paucity of the archaeological evidence, the absence of contemporary documents and the resurgence of barbarism help to emphasise the mystery of this period and the historian is obliged to rely on legends, folklore and place-names in order to interpret, albeit sketchily, the pattern of events. From early Welsh sources it appears that sometime in the fifth century a British Kingdom named Rheged emerged in the north-west; the boundaries are ill-defined though it is believed that the territory extended north of the Solway and probably as far as the river Duddon, though some authorities argue convincingly that the Ribble formed the southern boundary. The most important king of Rheged was Urien, a legendary and shadowy monarch, lionised by the Welsh bard Taliesin; he was said to have had his home at *Lywyfenedd* which is perhaps the district near the river Lyvennet in Westmorland. Urien's heroic exploits, and in particular the siege of the Anglian-held Lindisfarne in A.D. 574, ring down the centuries, but, following his death at the end of the century, the fortunes of his kingdom declined and it became subservient to the neighbouring kingdom of Strathclyde. It was during this period that the inhabitants of the enlarged kingdom of Strathclyde, together with those of Wales became known as *Cymry*, the compatriots, and from this ancient Celtic word the name Cumberland and Cumbria is derived as well as the Welsh word for Wales, *Cymru*.

The common unity between the Welsh and the Cumbrian Britons is further emphasised by place-name evidence; the modern Welsh elements *glyn* (valley), *pen* (head), *blaen* (top), *caer* (fortress) and *tor* (peak) are found in such Cumbrian place-names as Glencoyne and Glenderamakin, Pendruddock and Penrith, Blennerhasset and Blencathra, Caermote and Torpenhow. Moreover, many of the river names in Cumberland and Westmorland are Celtic in origin—the Derwent, Ehen, Esk, Irt, Mite, Calder and Kent. But perhaps the most intriguing piece of evidence for Cymric cultural unity is the well-known example of sheep scoring numerals; although dialect versions vary slightly between the major Lakeland valleys, nevertheless there are remarkable and distinct similarities between the numerals 1, 5, 10, 15 and 20, not only in Cumbria, and Old Welsh, but also in the old Cornish language and in Breton.

32 *Standing 10 feet high, the Irton Anglian cross, Cumberland, probably owes its fine state of preservation to its remote location.*

The early history of the Christian Church has a part in this story of Celtic Cumbria; indeed, if Cumberland can be said to have a 'county' saint, he must surely be St Kentigern, or, to give him his other name, Mungo. Although it has been argued that saints such as Patrick and Ninian undertook missions here at the end of the Roman occupation, their activities are ill-defined. The Kentigern legend, however, may have a basis in fact; sometime after A.D. 573 St Kentigern seems to have entered Cumberland on a mission from his Celtic Church in Glasgow, and preached at Crosfield, which can tentatively be identified with Crosthwaite, outside Keswick. Further support for this hypothesis might be found in a number of churches which were dedicated to Kentigern (Mungo); as well as the church at Crosthwaite, the list includes Caldbeck, Castle Sowerby, Mungrisdale, Grinsdale, Aspatria, Bromfield, and Irthington, east of Carlisle.

By the beginning of the 7th century the power of the *Cymry* declined in the face of a new threat—the expansion of the Anglian empire. During the reign of Aethelfrith (A.D. 593-617), the two Anglian kingdoms of Bernicia and Deira were welded together to form the powerful kingdom of Northumbria and this initiated a period of expansion. Following the Battle of Chester in A.D. 615 when Anglian forces successfully drove a wedge between the Celtic peoples of Wales and Cumbria, the colonisation movement accelerated dramatically, and by the end of the seventh century it seems that most of Cumbria was in their hands. Indeed, it is interesting to reflect that whereas the name Cumberland has its origin in the Celtic word *Cymry*, Westmorland is derived from the Anglian *Westmaringaland*, 'the land of the Western border', appropriate enough if one considers the Northumbrian point of view.

The absence of pagan Anglian burial grounds in Cumberland and Westmorland points to the fact that by the time they made their trek across the Pennines they had become Christian converts. Around the fringes of the Lake District uplands, fine examples of early Anglian sculptured stone crosses still survive, seen in positions they have occupied for 1,000 years. Churches at Addingham, Brigham, Carlisle, Dacre, Irton, Waberthwaite, Kendal, Kirkby Stephen, and Heversham all have examples, while late Anglian crosses can be seen at such places as Burton-in-Kendal, Beckermet, St Bees, Bromfield, Workington, Plumbland, and Dearham, and the

33 *Seventh-century Bewcastle cross.*

cylindrical cross-shafts in Penrith churchyard show signs of 10th-century Mercian influence. But the earliest and finest example of Anglian work-manship stands in St Cuthbert's churchyard at Bewcastle surrounded by some of the wildest, cloud-catching fells in England; described by the late Professor R.G. Collingwood as '... perhaps the first extant masterpiece of Early English stone carving', the vine-scrolls, figures, birds, and runic inscriptions are characteristic of Northumbrian workmanship. In spite of its decapitation and centuries of exposure to the harsh weathering in this bleak and isolated North Cumberland churchyard, the Bewcastle cross still stands, a mute but impressive witness not only to the skill of the craftsmen who carved it in the last decades of the seventh century, but also to the power of the new religion so recently accepted by the Anglian people.

34 *The figure of Christ, west face of Bewcastle cross.*

With the exception of the stone crosses, very few Anglian artefacts have been unearthed in Cumberland and Westmorland, and so far no Anglian houses or halls have been positively identified. This relative absence of archaeological evidence makes the remarkable Ormside bowl even more significant; the beautiful silver-gilt bowl, decorated with repoussé ornamen-tation, was found in Ormside churchyard near Appleby in 1823. Undoubt-edly one of the finest pieces of Anglian metalwork ever found in Northern England, it is believed to date from the late eighth century. In 1898 a ninth-century Scandinavian sword, shield-boss and knife were found at the same spot and it is tempting to suggest that the Ormside bowl was part of the loot of a pagan warrior returning home after the sack of the Anglian monastery at Dacre, or the destruction of Carlisle by Halfdan, the Danish King of York, in A.D.875.

If the remains of Anglian houses have left no trace on the landscape it is not really surprising; after all, the sites chosen by these farmers have been cultivated repeatedly during the last 1,000 years, and no doubt much evidence has been eradicated by the plough. Moreover, the original Anglian farmers chose well, for they established, together with the later Norse-Irish settlers, the present-day settlement pattern, and many of their original foun-dations took root in the fertile soils of the Eden Valley, the Cumbrian plain and the Westmorland lowlands to become the towns and villages of the 20th century. The scientific and sophisticated study of place-names has helped to illuminate the movements of the early Anglian colonists; some of the earliest settlements may be identified by the ending *-ingham* as in Addingham on the upper Eden, and Hensingham and Whicham (formerly Whittingham) on the Cumberland coastal plain. From these early nuclei a secondary stage of colonisation developed, indicated by *-ham* and *-ing(a) tun* endings such as Brigham, Dearham, Frizington, Workington and Harrington in Cumberland, and Askham, Heversham, Helsington, and Killington in Westmorland. The most frequent Anglian element in Cum-berland and Westmorland place-names is *-tun*, meaning a farmstead, and examples from the two counties are many: Waverton, Wigton, Irton, Hayton, Bampton, Clifton, Dufton, Burton, Murton, are characteristic.

35 *Part of the eighth-century Ormside bowl, one of the finest pieces of Anglian metal work ever found in the north of England.*

Any distribution of Anglian place-names will clearly demonstrate the concentration of settlement on the lower ground, usually below the 250-ft.

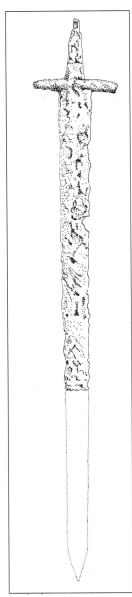

36 *Viking sword from Witherslack, Westmorland, now in the Kendal Museum.*

contour, and on the fertile loams and boulder clay of the Lake District margin; the Kent and the lower Lune valleys and the north-east or sunny side of the Eden Valley together with the Cumberland plain certainly seem to substantiate this thesis. Furthermore, there are few Anglian place-names within the Lake District uplands, for it seems that the new farming communities shunned the rugged, mist-shrouded fells with their high rainfall and stony, thin and acid soils.

Certainly by the end of the seventh century most of the land encircling the Lake District dome was under Anglian control, but what happened to the original inhabitants, the Cymric Britons? In some instances it seems that the native peoples were regarded as chattels to be transferred with land at the will of their Anglian master, for in A.D. 685 King Ecgfrith of Northumbria made a grant of lands to St Cuthbert which included territory in Carlisle together with Cartmel (formerly in North Lancashire) and all its British inhabitants—*et omnes Britannos cum eo*. However, this cannot be the complete picture for the predominance of Celtic place-names in the fells, particularly north and east of Carlisle and in the foothills between the river Eden and the northern hills of the Lake District dome, suggests that the British continued their pastoral way of life. Unhindered by their new overlords and unaware of the impending invasion of a new group of people from the west who would further change the settlement pattern of this north-western part of England, the Celts tended their sheep and goats for another 200 years.

Perhaps more than most peoples, the Vikings have acquired for themselves an unenviable public image. This is not surprising when one reflects that the history of the Vikings was written by their enemies, but even in the 20th century the Viking myth is perpetuated by Hollywood and the media, and the popular image of horn-helmeted heathens bringing fire, pillage, and slaughter to monastic houses and defenceless villages is a difficult one to erase. Of course, there can be little doubt that the early visits of the Scandinavians to Cumberland and Westmorland conformed to the stereotyped pattern, and no doubt these early raiders were roundly condemned by Christian scribes for, as Gwyn Jones rightly points out, '... the pain and grief of war incite the pen more than the tamer processes of trade'. However, there is another side to this coin; it must be remembered that, like the Anglians, the Scandinavians formed part of a folk movement of new settlers, but whereas the Anglian farmers sought and colonised the good quality soils, the Scandinavians were pastoralists and on the whole established themselves in the fells and along the creeks and inlets of the coast. These newcomers were also skilled craftsmen and examples of their carved stone crosses may be seen in several churches in the two counties, but in addition to their more tangible remains the Scandinavians have left a permanent impression on the place-names, the folk lore, and the dialect of Cumberland and Westmorland.

It is difficult to give a precise date for the movement of Scandinavian settlers into the area for this important phase in the history of north-west England has gone almost unrecorded, but by the second half of the ninth century the first settlers had arrived. It is a common but erroneous belief that the Vikings arrived in the dragon-powered long-ships directly from the *viks* or inlets of western Norway—in fact, the 'Vikings' who colonised Cumberland and Westmorland were second or third generation Scandinavians who came from Ireland and the Isle of Man, and as such they should be called Norse-Irish. Archaeological evidence indicates that the Vikings appeared in the Shetlands and the Orkneys about the middle of the eighth century, and from there they moved along the barren and rocky coastline of western Scotland and ultimately into the Irish Sea basin where, under their leader Olaf the White, they established themselves in the Dublin area and later extended their control to the Isle of Man. Here contact and intermarriage with Gaelic peoples brought about a remarkable and fruitful fusion of the two cultures, Norse and Irish, the results of which can be seen in the place-names and carved stone crosses of Cumberland and Westmorland.

Little is known of the actual migration of the Norse-Irish peoples from Ireland and the Isle of Man to Cumbria, but Professor W.G. Collingwood has argued convincingly that this movement was not of invaders, but of refugees. He bases his hypothesis on the *Heimskringla* saga of the Icelandic historian, Snorri Sturluson, which tells of the hostilities which developed between Harald Fairhair, King of Norway, and the Scandinavian colonists in Orkney, Shetland, the Hebrides, and Man, for it seems that the islanders had gone 'a-viking' in reverse—instead of raiding the British and Atlantic islands, they had the audacity to raid the Norwegian coasts! Such table-turning goaded Harald into launching an expedition against the rebels, and in A.D. 895 a fleet of viking ships from Norway harried the western sea-board of Scotland, but news of Harald's action reached Man before his warships and, according to Snorri, '... then fled all folk into Scotland, and the island was unpeopled of men: all goods that might be shifted and flitted away. So when Harald's folk went a-land there took they no booty'. Now the saga is quite specific about the refuge—it was Scotland, but Collingwood points out that Cumberland was, in fact, part of Scotland until William Rufus advanced on Carlisle in 1092, and although Snorri wrote the saga in the early 13th century, he was probably using the old political geography. It seems plausible, then, that the refugees from Harald Fairhair's wrath would flee to Cumbria; certainly they must have known the coastal area—after all, it is visible from the Isle of Man on a clear day, and, moreover, they probably had kinsmen settled there already. One further observation might be made to support the Collingwood thesis—the fact that along the Cumberland coastal plain Norse place-names occur in close proximity to earlier Anglian names and it could be argued that if these Norse-Irish peoples had come to Cumbria as hostile invaders, surely they would have destroyed the existing Anglian villages and so erased their place-names. This does not seem to have occurred, and this early example of racial harmony could perhaps reflect a peaceful influx of Norse-Irish refugees.

The map of central Lakeland bristles with Norse names—tarn *(tjörn)*, dale *(dalr)*, fell *(fjell)*, beck *(bekkr)*, and waterfall *(foss)* are all names

37 *Norse and Norse-Irish place-names in Cumberland and West-morland. Such names give useful indication of the distribution of Scandinavian settlement; names incorporating -saetr and -erg (Irish, -airigh) signify summer pastures. Based on information in* The Place Names of Cumberland, *1950, and* The Place Names of Westmorland, *1967.*

38 *The Dolphin runes, Carlisle Cathedral. Norse inscription, early 12th century.*

39 *A silver Norse-Irish penannular brooch found at Orton Scar, Westmorland, in 1847. Length: 11 inches.*

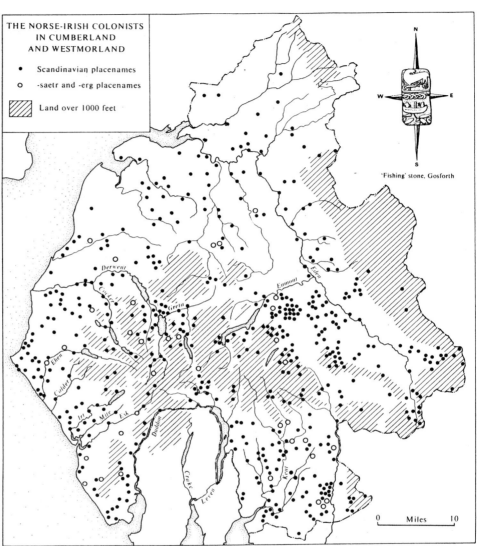

THE NORSE-IRISH COLONISTS IN CUMBERLAND AND WESTMORLAND

- Scandinavian placenames
○ -saetr and -erg placenames
▨ Land over 1000 feet

'Fishing' stone, Gosforth

0   Miles   10

which can be readily identified on any modern map of Norway or Iceland, while that most Scandinavian of place-names elements, thwaite *(tveit)*, meaning a clearing or enclosure in the woodland, is so common as to defy enumeration. Other place-names indicate the Irish origin of the Norse settlers—elements such as *erg* or *airigh* from the Irish word for a summer pasture are found in such names as Mosser, Birker and Cleator in Cumberland, and Mansergh and Sizergh in Westmorland; elsewhere, however, the pure Scandinavian word for a summer pasture, *saeter*, is found in such names as Seatoller (the seater among the alder trees), Ambleside (Hamal's saeter), Seathwaite (the clearing with the saeter), and Arnside (Arni's saeter).

But more than mere place-names were influenced by the Norse-Irish people, for even as late as the 12th century masons were carving

Scandinavian runic inscriptions on their memorials—and in all probability the people of this remote area of north-west England were speaking a form of Old Norse. Some of the evidence for this assertion can still be seen; during the restoration of Carlisle cathedral in 1855 a piece of runic graffiti was found which reads, 'Dolfin wrote these runes on this stone', an inscription which is pure Norse and which dates from the early 12th century. A somewhat later runic inscription on the font in Bridekirk church is a mixture of Scandinavian and early English suggesting that by the second half of the 12th century a cultural fusion was taking place. Moreover, the Scandinavian impact on the folk speech of Cumbria is clearly apparent to the careful listener, for this dialect, aptly described by the Cumberland poet, Norman Nicholson, as a 'clicking, cracking, harshly melodious tune', contains many words which would be readily recognised by a Norwegian or an Icelander.

40 *The 'Bound Devil', Kirkby Stephen, Westmorland—perhaps an illustration of the punishment of the Norse god, Loki.*

On the whole, Cumberland and Westmorland have few examples of pagan Viking burials and there are no known cases of the boat burials which so fire the imagination in Norway and the Isle of Man; the paucity of such graves may indicate that by the time the Norse-Irish people arrived here they had already been largely converted to Christianity. However, perhaps there were some who did not lightly abandon Odin, Thor and the rest of the gods in the Norse pantheon for pagan warrior graves, complete with swords and other equipment, have been found at such places as Seaton, near Workington, Aspatria, and Eaglesfield, while the grave goods of a cremation burial at Hesket-in-the-Forest included a sword with a hilt-mount engraved with the same chain-pattern found on Scandinavian crosses in the Isle of Man and Cumberland. In addition, a few silver brooches have been found at such places as Orton Scar, Brayton Hall, near Aspatria, and at a site near Penrith, but the most outstanding discovery was made at Fluskew Pike, north of Dacre, in 1785—it was a magnificent 'thistle' brooch with a pin some 22 ins. long. It can be seen today in the British Museum, a noble example of the Norse silversmith's skill.

If the archaeological evidence of the Norse-Irish settlers is disappointing, their sculptured crosses are of special interest for many of them combine pure Scandinavian workmanship with Irish characteristics. Examples of such crosses may be seen at such places as Muncaster, Brigham, Dearham, Aspatria, Gilcrux, Bromfield, Rockcliffe, Penrith, and Kirkby Stephen, but the finest of all stands in the churchyard at Gosforth. Rivalled in interest only by the Anglian cross at Bewcastle, the Gosforth Cross was carved at the end of the 10th century or the beginning of the 11th and the symbolism on this slender sandstone pillar represents a curious fusion of Norse pagan mythology and Christian beliefs. The lower part of the wheel-headed cross represents the sacred world ash tree, Yggdrasil, but the four panels of the upper shaft are carved with scenes illustrating the poetic *Edda*, that epic story of Ragnarök, the struggle between Odin and the other gods against the powers of evil. Here in this quiet West Cumberland churchyard may be seen the mischievous Loki, bound hand and foot and cast into a pit for his part in the slaying of Balder; Heimdal, who guarded the rainbow bridge to

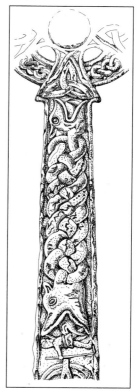

41 *Detail from the Gosforth Cross. Vidar fighting the Fenris wolf.*

42 *Gosforth Cross: The Crucifixion.*

Asgard, shown with his horn in his left hand ready to sound the alarm, while Vidar, the sole survivor of the old gods, bravely fights the evil Fenris wolf, represented on the cross by a double-headed dragon. All these symbols would be familiar to a people steeped in Norse mythology and tradition, but also shown on the east side of the cross is the unmistakable representation of the Crucifixion and it seems that the message of the Gosforth Cross relates to the passing of the old pagan gods and the arrival of the Christ who overcame the forces of darkness.

Within the church at Gosforth are several other carved stones which show clear Norse workmanship, notably the famous 'Fishing Stone' which illustrates the popular Norse legend of how Thor tried to catch the evil Midgard Serpent but, like many a fisherman, failed to land his catch. The same episode is shown on sculptured stones at Altuna in Sweden and Thisted in Denmark. The two house-shaped hog-back stones also preserved inside the church are outstanding examples of this type of Norse tombstone; the most famous of the two is the so-called 'two armies' hog-back on the side of which two groups of men armed with spears and round shields face each other.

So far no examples of Viking longhouses have come to light, probably for the same reason that no Anglian houses have been found—the Scandinavians chose their settlement sites carefully and in so doing they chose the locations of the present towns and villages, sites which have been built on for centuries. But what became of the Norse saeters, those summer pastures and huts at the heads of the Cumbrian dales? Some, of course, became permanent settlement sites, others probably remained in use as saeters for centuries before the small stone-built huts finally fell into disuse.

43 *The terraced mound behind Fell Foot Farm, Little Langdale, Westmorland. Making the comparison with Tynwald Hill at St Johns in the Isle of Man, Professor W.G. Collingwood declared that '... this thingmount in Little Langdale may be regarded as the Lakeland Tynwald'. If he was correct, we have here one of the most remarkable monuments of the Norse-Irish colonisation of Cumberland and Westmorland.*

Several have been tentatively identified, but the whole problem of early medieval saeters remains to be investigated.

It is possible that as well as introducing their crafts, skills and language to Cumberland and Westmorland, the Norse-Irish settlers brought something else—their system of assemblies or 'things' where men gathered to elect a 'law speaker' and where the new laws were proclaimed before the assembled people. In the Isle of Man the tradition is proudly maintained, and on 5 July every year the Tynwald ceremony is held at the terraced mound at St John's. There are no records of such 'things' being held in Cumberland and Westmorland, although the former place-name 'Thengeheved' near Shap may indicate such a thingmount. However, observant fell walkers can still pick out the remains of a square, terraced mound behind the farm at Fell Foot in Little Langdale. It has been argued that the terracing was part of a garden, though the theory is unlikely, and any comparison between the Little Langdale mound and Tynwald Hill in the Isle of Man must surely underline the close parallels which exist; indeed, that eminent Anglo-Norse scholar, Professor W.G. Collingwood, concluded that '... this thingmount in Little Langdale may be regarded as the Lakeland Tynwald'. If he was correct in his interpretation, we have here in this Westmorland dale a truly remarkable memorial to our Norse-Irish ancestors.

44 *The 'Fishing Stone', Gosforth, Cumberland.*

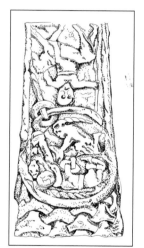

45 *Detail from Gosforth Cross: the punishment of Loki.*

4

Border Barons and Medieval Monasteries

The entire course of English history was irrevocably changed at Hastings on 14 October 1066, when the Norman cavalry broke through the 'shield wall' of the Saxon Housecarls, so snatching victory for Duke William of Normandy. In Cumberland and Westmorland, however, the hostilities at Hastings meant nothing, for in 1066 the area was debatable land, shuttlecocked between England and Scotland and this situation continued into the 12th century. The political history of the borderlands during the century preceding 1066 is complicated not only by the Norse-Irish colonisation, but also by a resurgence of the British Kingdom of Strathclyde. During the reign of Edward the Confessor the famous Gospatrick's Writ was issued; this is the earliest document to deal with Cumberland, and although the surviving manuscript is a 13th-century transcript, nevertheless it is an important source of information. From the wording of the document it seems that during the second half of the ninth century the district roughly defined by the Derwent, the Eamont, the central fells and the marshes at the head of the Solway was covered by the phrase 'the lands that were Cumbrian' and this seems to indicate that this area, which had been Anglian from the early seventh century until the early 10th century, had been Cumbrian for a considerable part of the following century and a half. It would appear, then, that during the 10th century, Anglian influence declined and that part of Cumbria as far south as Eamont once again came under the control of Strathclyde.

For a time, the river Eamont seems to have been the frontier between the English and the people of Strathclyde but by the middle of the 10th century the balance of power changed again. In A.D.945 Duvenald or Dunmail of Strathclyde was defeated in battle by King Edmund of Northumbria and, following the British defeat, Cumbria was handed over to Malcolm I of Scotland on the understanding that he lent his support to the English king whenever it was required. It remained part of Scotland until 1032 when King Cnut (Canute) exchanged Lothian for Cumbria, but perhaps before 1066, and certainly by 1068, all the lands north of the Derwent and the Eamont had been seized by the Scots under Malcolm III and once again the boundary of Scotland lay across the dome of the Lake District. As a direct result of this, almost the whole of Cumberland and a large part of Westmorland are not included in the Domesday survey of 1086 simply because they lay on the Scottish side of the border.

If 1066 was of little significance to Cumberland and Westmorland, 1092, on the other hand, was a year of reckoning, for the period of Scottish domination was abruptly terminated and the balance of power redressed in England's favour. The Anglo-Saxon Chronicle relates how, in that year, the Conqueror's son, William II, 'marched north to Carlisle with a large army, and re-established the fortress, and built the castle, and drove out Dolfin who had previously ruled the land there, and garrisoned the castle with his men, and afterwards returned to the south, and sent thither very many peasants with their wives and stock to dwell there to till the ground'. Politically, of course, this was a sound move, for William II, like the Romans, had decided to make the Solway the frontier between his own kingdom and Scotland; moreover, his policy of planting English settlers in the region may have been motivated by more than a desire to increase the productivity of the area and it can be argued that he wished to have in his newly-acquired territory people whose loyalties he could trust. Exactly what William II found when he entered Carlisle is open to conjecture; if a town existed at all before 1092 then it seems likely that it occupied the higher ground now covered by the cathedral, St Cuthbert's church and the area to the south along the line of Blackfriars Street. If, as the Anglo-Saxon Chronicle states, William built the castle, it would almost certainly be a motte-and-bailey structure, a palisaded wooden building surmounting an artificial hill, rather than the stone building which can be seen today.

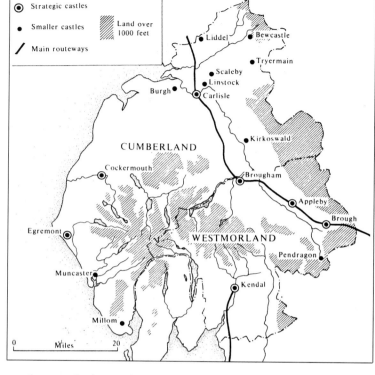

46 *12th- and 13th-century castles in Cumberland and Westmorland.*

Undoubtedly William Rufus's occupation of Carlisle marks a turning point in the history of the north-west of England, for it brought this area within the Norman sphere of influence, yet, despite the new fortifications, the Norman hold on the borders did not go unchallenged. During Henry I's reign the castle was strengthened, but following his death in 1135 the Scots took advantage of the anarchy of Stephen's troubled reign; David, King of Scotland, sent his troops across the border to support his niece, Matilda, in her claim to the throne, and yet again most of Cumberland and Westmorland became Scottish and Carlisle became a Scottish city with a Scots garrison in its castle. Clearly anxious to keep out the English, the Scots strengthened the city's defences, raised the height of the city walls, and almost certainly constructed the present square keep of the castle.

David of Scotland died in Carlisle Castle in 1153 and was succeeded by his grandson, Malcolm the Maiden, who lacked the power to hold his English lands, and four years later Henry II seized back Cumberland and Westmorland and granted Carlisle its first charter as an English city. William the Lion succeeded his brother Malcolm as King of Scotland in 1165 and promptly challenged Henry's claim to Carlisle; in 1174 he crossed the border with a force said to have numbered 80,000 men and besieged the castle for three months, but, ironically, such was the strength of his grandfather's defences that the siege was not successful. Yet still the Scottish claims were pressed; during the domestic crises which marked King John's reign, the Scots King, Alexander II, crossed the border and in 1216 took the city of Carlisle and its castle. The occupation was short-lived, for John died in that year and his successor, Henry III, ordered Alexander to retire to Scotland which he did—but not without financial compensation. From this time until the present—with the exception of a brief occupation by the Young Pretender—Carlisle has remained an English city.

Turning from the tortuous politics of Anglo-Scottish feuds to the Norman administration of the newly-captured lands, it appears that in true feudal fashion the border regions were reorganised under powerful barons who were responsible for the defence of the area. Although the lack of documents makes the unravelling of the political machinations difficult, it is clear that at the beginning of the 12th century the most important figure was Ranulph de Briquessart, usually known as Ranulph de Meschines; to him was given 'the land of Carlisle' which comprised the area around the

47 *The medieval seal of the City of Carlisle.*

city and the lower Eden valley. In addition, Ranulf also acquired the Barony of Appleby which included much of the upper Eden valley. Next in the Norman hierarchy was Ivo Taillebois, who received a grant of the estates of the Kendal barony from William II, but, on the marriage of his daughter to Ranulf de Meschines, the estates passed to Ranulf, thereby increasing his territory and authority. For 25 years Ranulf ruled his border empire until, in 1120, he succeeded to the Earldom of Chester and relinquished his northern territories which returned once more to the Crown. In the resulting reallocation of the territories the Crown retained Carlisle and its region together with the Forest of Inglewood, but West Cumberland was divided into two fiefs, Allerdale below Derwent and Allerdale above Derwent or Copeland, a name derived from the Old Norse word *kaupaland*, meaning 'bought land'. Along the border three small baronies, Gilsland, Liddel and Burgh-by-Sands had been parcelled out by Ranulf and to these Henry I added Levington and Wigton, and in central Cumberland the barony of Greystoke was created, while in Westmorland geography dictated that two units be established—Appleby and Kendal. Finally the whole of this northern territory was divided into two sheriffdoms called Caerliolum (the name Cumberland was not used until 1177) and Westmarieland, and this marks the genesis of the two separate counties.

By the middle of the 12th century, then, the political framework of the marchlands had been established and by this time, too, the system of castles and fortifications which was the key to the border had developed. There are no early Norman castles within the fells, but in the fertile Eden valley, Kentdale, and the Cumberland coastal plain, there they can be found. At Brougham and Brough the Norman builders constructed their castles amid the remains of ancient Roman forts, but at Appleby they chose a new site within a meander loop of the Eden. Along the border, castles were built at Burgh, Liddell, Brampton, Irthington, and later, Naworth and these, together with the castle at Carlisle, formed the first line of defence. On the Cumberland coastal lowlands the two most important Norman castles were at Cockermouth and Egremont. Many of these castles began as simple motte-and-bailey constructions which were later rebuilt in stone, while in other cases the original motte was abandoned and another site chosen; at Kendal the original motte-and-bailey of the de Lancaster family still dominates the western part of the town, faced, on the eastern bank of the Kent, by the equally dominating 13th-century stone-built castle perched on the summit of a boulder-clay mound.

However, the Norman castles are only one aspect in the evolution of the early medieval landscape, for the policy of introducing new colonists initiated by William II was further encouraged. Once again the paucity of documentary evidence makes it necessary to rely on place-names and in particular those names which combine a Norman personal name with -by. Examples are common in the Carlisle area—Botcherby, Etterby, Harraby, Upperby, Tarraby, Aglionby—but there are also three names of this type in the Greystoke area—Johnby, Ellonby, and Lamonby. Clearly, new settlements such as these in an otherwise remote and inhospitable border area helped to improve the economic fortunes of the region as well as providing a political bulwark against the Scots. But there were other areas in which the Norman overlords actively discouraged colonisation or the expansion of existing settlements; although these areas were known as 'forests', it is wrong to regard them as woodland areas—they were, in fact, tracts of land in which the harsh forest laws prevailed. To the Norman kings and their followers, the chase was everything; in a way it was an extension of warfare, and consequently huge areas were set aside for hunting. In these forest areas the deer was held in greater esteem than people, and the penalties for poaching were severe. Within Cumberland and Westmorland there are several extensive private forests including Sleddale Forest, Fawcett Forest, Thornthwaite Forest, Ralfland Forest, Copeland Forest, Derwentfells Forest, and Skiddaw Forest, most of them occupying the thinly-populated mountainous areas. Inglewood Forest, however, was the exception; this was a royal forest reserved exclusively for the king's hunting, and, moreover, it was the most extensive hunting ground in England. Stretching from the slopes of Crossfell to Bowness-on-Solway, and from there to Crosthwaite near Keswick, it measured about 40 miles from east to west, and 25 miles north to south. Some estimation of the game within the forest can be gathered by the fact that, during Henry III's reign, 200 harts and the same number of hinds were killed in two successive years, while Edward I, visiting Inglewood in 1279, slaughtered 400 harts and hinds in one day. Extraordinary care was taken to protect the animals, and consequently Henry II

48 *13th-century seal of the Borough of Appleby.*

excluded from his forest anyone having bows and arrows or dogs; no forest land was to be cultivated and the felling of trees or the building of huts or shelters was forbidden. With such stringent limitations to settlement it is not surprising that Inglewood remained an isolated and backward area until the 16th century.

If some areas suffered under a restrictive forest code, others flourished and thriving market towns developed under the patronage of the Norman barons. At Appleby, where Ranulph de Meschines had built his castle on a virgin site, a new town came into existence in 1110 and in 1179 it received its first charter, built the splendid church of St Lawrence, and became a centre of trade. In West Cumberland a new town with a Norman-French name, Egremont, was planned and laid out between 1130 and 1140 by William de Meschines, Lord of Copeland and brother of Ranulph. In 1189 Gilbert fitz Reinfred obtained a grant of a charter for Kendal and in so doing assured the prosperity of the town, while Penrith, which had a market as early as 1123, prospered as the commercial centre of the Honour of Penrith. Even in the remote north-eastern Barony of Gilsland, the lords of Gilsland decreed that Brampton should become the market centre for their territory, and in the 13th century another new town, Cockermouth, grew up in the shadow of the castle walls.

If the 12th century was a period of consolidation and colonisation in Cumberland and Westmorland, it was also one of religious fervour. Just as the Conqueror himself endowed a monastery at Battle as a thanksgiving offering for his victory at Hastings, so, too, his followers also established religious houses in their newly-acquired territories. Although these tough, ruthless Norman barons were not sentimental, they were deeply religious; they feared death, Hell, and Purgatory and firmly believed that the endowment of a monastery would benefit their everlasting souls, thereby obtaining good value from their investment! However the Normans did not allow their religious zeal to overcome their business acumen for, as W.G. Collingwood explains, '... when the early Norman lords had grants of perfectly wild country where the people were so rough that it did not seem likely they would pay their rents, the natural impulse was to give a

49 *Lanercost Priory, Cumberland, was founded in 1166 by Robert de Vaux, Lord of Gilsland, for Augustinian Canons. It lies in the beautiful, secluded Irthing valley, within sight of Hadrian's Wall.*

good piece to the priests'. This, in part, explains the apparent generosity of the Norman barons to the Church; they could not have foreseen the influence the monasteries would have on the human landscape of Cumberland and Westmorland. Following the established pattern, Ranulph de Meschines founded a small Benedictine priory at Wetheral some time between 1106 and 1112 and a few years later, in 1120, his brother William, Lord of Copeland, established another Benedictine house at St Bees. In 1122 or 1123, probably at the suggestion of Thurston, Archbishop of York, Henry I founded an Augustinian house at Carlisle and in 1127 Henry's nephew, Stephen, Count of Boulogne and later King of England, established the Abbey of St Mary of Furness, later to become one of the most powerful Cistercian abbeys in the country and owner of considerable areas of land within Cumberland. In 1134 a daughter abbey to Furness was established in the secluded valley of the Calder on land which had been given to the Cistercians by another Ranulph de Meschines, son of the founder of St Bees. In 1150, at a time when Cumberland was more Scottish than English, Prince Henry, son of David I of Scotland, founded Holm Cultram Abbey, a daughter house to Melrose in Roxburghshire, and shortly after, in 1166, Robert de Vaux, Lord of Gilsland, established the Augustinian priory at Lanercost in the remote but beautiful Irthing valley. The last monastery to be endowed—and the only Norman abbey within Westmorland—was the Premonstratensian house at Shap; originally founded at Preston Patrick by Thomas, son of Gospatric, the community moved to the bleak Shap fells around 1199. The isolated and half-wild border marchland can hardly have afforded an hospitable environment for the intrepid communities of monks and, indeed, it must have been a positively dangerous location for nuns, yet such was the power of Norman monasticism that two small nunneries were established in the last years of the 12th century, one at Seaton near Bootle in West Cumberland, and the other at Armathwaite on the Eden.

With the sole exception of Shap, all the Norman monasteries lay outside the mountain core of the Lake District, yet several of them held territory within the upland. St Bees owned the chapels of Eskdale, Ennerdale and Loweswater as well as the Manor of Ennerdale and the fells above Loweswater and also had the right of pannage for swine in these western dales; Carlisle Priory held land in the Vale of Lorton and Shap owned land in the fells east of Ullswater. Reflecting its Scottish connections, Holm Cultram held land in Galloway and southern Scotland, but also had scat-

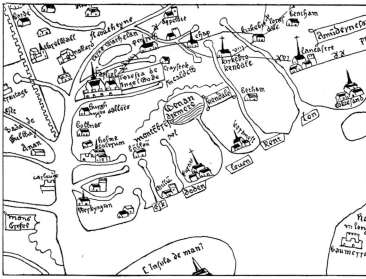

50 *Part of the Gough map—a 14th-century picture of Cumbria. The rivers Lune, Kent, Leven, Duddon, Esk and Eden are named as are the towns of Carlisle, Penrith, Appleby, Kendal, Kirkby Lonsdale and Workington. In addition, the monastic houses at Shap, Holm Cultram, Furness and Cartmel are shown, and fortified towers are marked at Appleby, Brough and Millom, while Carlisle is distinguished by the priory and fortifications. Windermere, the Cumbrian mountains, the Forest of Inglewood and Hadrian's Wall are indicated, and the main roads are marked by a single black line, with distances between towns in Roman numerals.*

51 *Monk's Bridge over the river Calder, Cumberland. This single-arch structure, lacking walls or parapets, is a good example of a pack-horse bridge. Such bridges are notoriously difficult to date though there is a strong tradition that this one was built by the monks of nearby Calder Abbey.*

tered holdings on the Solway plain, in the Eden valley and within the Cumberland fells. As well as the Cumberland and Westmorland monasteries, other religious houses also held land within the two counties. The most important was Furness, for as well as acquiring all the land between the east shore of Coniston water and the western shore of Windermere, Furness Abbey owned a large part of Borrowdale, bought in 1209 from Alice II de Rumelli, the heiress of Allerdale, for £156 13s. 4d., and at Grange-in-Borrowdale they established their home farm. In 1242 they added another 14,000 acres to their already extensive Cumberland property when they exchanged one of their farms at Monkfoss, near Bootle, for the boulder-strewn wilderness of Upper Eskdale, a transaction which, on the face of it, can hardly have benefited the monastery; in fact the monks acquired an important sheep-run and their grange at Brotherilkeld became one of their major sheep farms. Another important Cistercian monastery, Fountains in Yorkshire, also owned land within Cumberland, for it acquired the church and mill at Crosthwaite, near Kendal, Hestholm (Derwent Island in Derwentwater), Watendlath, Langstrath, and Stonethwaite. It was this latter property which gave rise to a celebrated, un-Christianlike wrangle between Fountains and Furness, which also laid claim to Stonethwaite. In 1304 Edward I confiscated the tiny property. Not to be outdone, the Abbot of Fountains, with true Yorkshire hard-headedness, offered the king 40 shillings for the property and was successful. A third Yorkshire Cistercian abbey owned land within the fells—Byland received a grant of part of the Westmorland Borrowdale from William II de Lancaster in 1180, and even the small Augustinian priory at Conishead in Furness held an estate at Baysbrown in Langdale.

It has been said, with some justification, that if the Norsemen stubbed the waste, the Normans brought it into cultivation. Certainly in the 12th and 13th centuries this process continued apace; the monastic communities—

IV *Askham, Westmorland. Clustered round a wide green, the village is an excellent example of a nucleated Anglian settlement. The shell of Robert Smirke's spectacular early 19th-century Lowther Castle forms an impressive backdrop.*

V *Brotherilkeld, Eskdale, Cumberland. In 1242 the Cistercian Abbey of St Mary of Furness acquired some 14,000 acres of land in upper Eskdale and built a grange or home farm at Brotherilkeld. The present farm probably stands on the original monastic site.*

VI *Sizergh Castle, Westmorland, is one of the most impressive houses in the north of England. The massive embattled tower is the pele constructed about 1340 as a defence against Scottish raids. Its walls are 9¾ feet thick at the base, tapering to 5½ feet at the top.*

VII *The Abbey of St Mary Magdalene, Shap, Westmorland. Shap Abbey was founded by the White Canons, the Premonstratensians, who moved here from Preston Patrick, near Kendal, around 1199. Most of the ruins date from the 13th century, but the western tower was constructed about 1500. Shap was suppressed in 1540, the last of the Cumbrian abbeys to be dissolved.*

52 *The font in St Bridget's Church at Bridekirk has been described by Nikolaus Pevsner as one of the liveliest pieces of Norman sculpture in Cumberland. Although it dates from the mid-12th century, it has an inscription in debased Scandinavian runes which reads 'Richard he me wrought, and to this beauty eagerly me brought'. Richard can be seen, completing his work with his chisel and mallet, underneath the inscription.*

and in particular the Cistercians—created huge sheep-walks in the fells, built *vaccaries* or dairy farms, and established home farms or granges. The Cistercian monks of Holm Cultram carried out extensive reclamation of marshes and mossland around Abbey Town and before the end of the 12th century granges had been established at Raby, Skinburness, Newton Arlosh and Mawbray. The destruction of the woodland gained momentum as more and more charcoal was required for the smelting of iron ore in crude bloomery furnaces, and more and more land was brought under cultivation. In the Newlands valley near Keswick the shallow Husaker tarn was drained and the land reclaimed for agriculture, so giving the valley its name; the present Uzzicar Farm is an interesting reminder of the former tarn. In short, then, the period up to the end of the 13th century was one of continuing colonisation and consolidation; however, the *Ragnarök* of the 14th-century Scottish wars and disastrous pestilences brought a halt to such development in the two counties.

53 *Medieval comfort. 'February', one of a series of carvings on the capitals in Carlisle Cathedral.*

5

The Turbulent Border

54 *The illuminated capital 'E' from Edward II's charter to Carlisle granted in 1316. The illustration shows Sir Andrew de Harcla, identified by his shield, in the act of defending the city walls against a Scottish attack.*

The destruction by fire of Carlisle cathedral choir in 1292 was a dismal omen which heralded a long, melancholy period in the history of Cumberland and Westmorland, a century prompted by plagues and famines, by lootings and invasions. The Black Death ravaged the two counties in 1348, 1361 and again in 1362, but even the natural disaster of plague was overshadowed by the man-made catastrophe of war, for the 14th century is marked by the festering Anglo-Scottish disputes which often broke out into open conflict.

Of all the English monarchs, Edward I's name stands out in the troubled history of the Border region; he alone was determined to impose English sovereignty on Scotland and to this end he made Carlisle an important military base as well as a centre of government, and parliaments were held in the castle in 1298, 1300 and 1307. Not unnaturally, the Scots resisted the English claim, and in 1296 the Earl of Buchan assembled 40,000 Scots, marched across the border, burned Lanercost and laid unsuccessful siege to Carlisle. Such a provocative act precipitated retaliation, and, in June 1300, Edward moved north to Carlisle and besieged Caerlaverock Castle in Dumfries, justly earning his nickname 'the hammer of the Scots'. Border defences were now improved and even churches were fortified as refuges; at Newton Arlosh, built in 1304, the main doorway was barely two feet seven inches wide, and none of the windows measures more than one foot in width or three foot four inches in height. Nearby, at Burgh-by-Sands, the church had two towers each with walls seven feet thick. Clearly both villages feared surprise attacks by Scots using the 'waths' or fords across the Solway, but other areas were equally vulnerable; although of a later date, the church tower at Great Salkeld in the Eden Valley was built in such a way that it could serve as a fort in time of strife.

55 *A crowned head, believed to be that of Edward I. From a carving in Carlisle Cathedral.*

After the capture and execution of that remarkable Scots guerrilla leader, William Wallace, it seemed inevitable that Scottish ambitions would be extinguished, but such was not to be, for Robert Bruce revived the Wallace tradition and in March 1306 he was crowned king; Scotland discovered in him a patriot and a leader—but Cumberland found a scourge. Under the pretext that Bruce had sworn fealty to the English crown and was therefore a traitor, Edward once again set out with his army for the border but by this time he was a tired and sick old man. Seized with dysentery, he was obliged to spend some time at Lanercost in the care of the monks, but by March

1307 he had recovered sufficiently to hold a parliament in Carlisle. However, the sands were running out for Edward; carried on a litter, the ailing monarch led his army out of Carlisle, intending to cross the Solway by the fords, but near Burgh, within sight of Scotland, he died on 7 July 1307.

Edward's feckless son, now Edward II, was a very different man from his father. After a token expedition across the border, he hastily withdrew to London leaving Cumberland to defend itself against Scottish retribution as best it could. The invasion came in 1311 when Bruce severely damaged Lanercost, but no help was forthcoming from the English Crown, and impoverished Cumberland had to buy off the Scots with hostages rather than money. When Edward finally bestirred himself, the result was Bannockburn where the English forces were routed and where Cumberland's fate was sealed. Encouraged by his victory, Bruce invaded England in November 1314, first devastating Northumberland before descending on Stainmore and destroying Brough, Appleby, and Kirkoswald. In the following year the Scots laid siege to Carlisle but failed to take the city because of the stout defence of Sir Andrew de Harcla; for his action he was made Earl of Carlisle in 1322, but soon lost the Royal favour and was accused of negotiating a peace treaty with Robert Bruce; it seems likely, in fact, that he recognised the futility of the seemingly endless struggle and was aware of the sufferings of the people. Whatever the rights and wrongs of the situation, in 1323 Sir Andrew was sentenced and hanged at Harraby outside Carlisle, his head was sent to London, and other fragments of his body were despatched to Carlisle, Newcastle and York. Ironically, Edward was forced to make a truce with the Scots in the same year.

In 1315 Copeland was ravaged, Egremont devastated and the churches of St Bees and Calder damaged, while in the following year the Scots penetrated as far as Richmond and Furness. The woeful account written by

56 *'A strong tower is our god.' St Cuthbert's Church, Great Salkeld, Cumberland. The broad western tower was built about 1380 to serve not only as a bell tower but as a pele tower in time of danger. Similar defensive church towers may be seen at Burgh-by-Sands and Newton Arlosh.*

57 *Edward II, from a woodcut by Thomas Bewick.*

58 *The arms of Sir Andrew de Harcla, defender of Carlisle.*

the Bishop of Carlisle during the early 14th century is a harsh reminder of the devastations; it tells of villages and towns burned, churches destroyed, treasure carried off, men, women and children slaughtered—a picture starkly reminiscent of the Anglian Church's reaction to the Viking raids centuries before. But this was no exaggerated account; moreover, these raids had more than a mere transitory effect for they brought in their wake depletion of livestock and grain, and privation and pestilence often followed. One sure indication of the effects of the Scottish raids can be found in the valuation of church property assessed for the purposes of papal taxation; within the diocese of Carlisle in 1291 the total valuation amounted to £3,171 5s. 7°d. but, following the wave of destructive raids, the valuation in 1318 was a mere £480 19s. 0d. But worse was yet to come.

In 1322 the Scots flooded over the border in greater force than ever before; after plundering the manor of Rose, south of Carlisle, they then moved to Holm Cultram Abbey which they devastated, despite its Scottish connections and also the fact that it contained the tomb of Robert Bruce's father. On into Allerdale and Copeland the raiders swept, burning and pillaging in a whirlwind of destruction. The Duddon Sands were crossed without opposition and Abbot John of Furness, fearing for his life and the property of his house, paid ransom in the hope that the Scots would respect the monastic territories; his hopes were thwarted, however, for much damage was done in Furness and in Cartmel where the priory was partly destroyed. Bruce and his army then crossed the sands of Morecambe Bay and, joining forces with another Scottish force, led by the Earl of Moray and Sir James Douglas, they attacked and looted Lancaster before proceeding on to Preston. There they turned north again and made for the border. The 'Great Raid' lasted three weeks and three days, and the resulting damage, destruction, and loss of life was enormous, and it was after this holocaust that Sir Andrew de Harcla made his private, but ill-starred, treaty with Robert Bruce. This Scottish invasion needed no monkish chronicler to record the lugubrious details on parchment—they were written on the Cumberland landscape and in the memories of men for the next half century.

In the following decades an uneasy peace settled on the borders, but in 1345 a Scottish army of over 30,000 men was once again in northern England. In 1380, 1385 and again in 1387 Carlisle was besieged and the surrounding countryside laid waste, and on 26 December 1388 Appleby was almost completely destroyed. So great was the destruction that the town never again achieved its former prosperity though it remained Westmorland's county town until the county itself was dissolved in 1974. It seems likely that in the same raid Brougham Castle was also destroyed since in 1403 an inquisition reported that 'it is worth nothing because it lieth waste by reason of the destruction by the Scots'; it remained so until repaired in the 17th century by that remarkable castle-restorer, Lady Anne Clifford.

The mood of uncertainty and suspicion which dominated the two counties in the 14th century found expression in the domestic architecture

59 *The church at Abbeytown, Cumberland, which incorporates the remaining parts of the Cistercian abbey of Holm Cultram. The abbey was devastated by the Scots in 1322 in spite of the fact that it contained the tomb of Robert Bruce's father.*

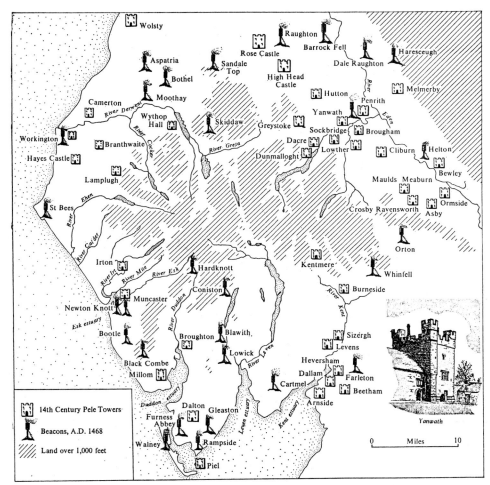

60 *The map shows pele towers built during the 14th century and beacons in 1468. With the exception of Kentmere and Burneside, the pele towers are located on the perimeter of the Lake District dome. The 12th-century castles at Kendal, Egremont, Appleby and Cockermouth are not shown on this map.*

Yanwath

0 Miles 10

61 *Four-square, turreted and crenellated, Dacre Castle, Cumberland, began as a 14th-century pele tower built by Ranulph de Dacre.*

62 *Thought to have been built in 1322 by John de Sutton, Yanwath pele tower, south of Penrith, is a good example of the type of refuge tower which proliferated in the 14th and 15th centuries in response to Scottish raids.*

of the area for this is the period when most of the fortified pele towers were built. Designed to withstand short sieges, these peles usually consisted of three storeys—the tunnel-vaulted ground floor which had no windows, a second floor which was often a hall with small windows and sometimes a fireplace, and a third floor which was generally a bower. Thick-set and built of stone, the walls varied in thickness from three feet to ten feet, and the roof was normally flat to allow arrows to be fired at raiders and missiles hurled down on unwanted visitors. In the event of a sudden attack, the owner, his family and some of his livestock could take refuge in the pele and these simple but sturdy towers, together with an 'early warning system' of beacon fires on prominent hills, undoubtedly gave some measure of protection to those affluent enough to be able to provide this form of defence. Today most of these peles have undergone additions and modifications; some, such as Kentmere Hall and Yanwath Hall, are simply part of a working farm, used for the storage of hay and farm machinery; others, such as Muncaster, Dacre or Sizergh castles, are now stately homes. A glance at a distribution map clearly indicates the most vulnerable districts, for there is a marked concentration in the Eden Valley, the Solway lowlands near to the fords, the West Cumberland coastal plain, and the Kent valley. Despite romantic and persistent legends of Scottish raiders swooping

down from the fells along Scots Rake
to attack Troutbeck, there is no evidence whatever that such raids
occurred within the Lake District upland, because it was unlikely that
these remote dales possessed anything
worth plundering! In any case, if the
Scots did happen to penetrate the
mountain fastness, the dalesfolk
could always seek refuge in the
bracken and screes of their fellsides.
In one or two cases, however, certain families preferred to be cautious,
and peles such as Kentmere Hall and
Yewbarrow Hall in Long Sleddale
are hidden away in their valleys,
exceptions which prove the rule.

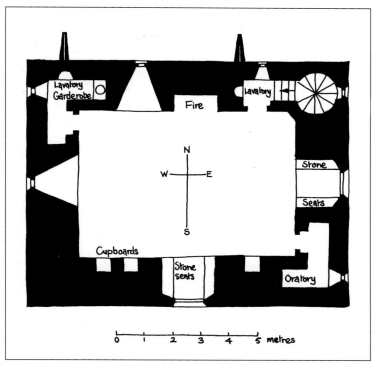

By the beginning of the 15th
century the chaos and uncertainties
of the previous century had receded
somewhat; the Scots raided less fre-
quently, and the great age of fortified towers was over, though peles
such as Blencow Hall were built. In
1463 Edward IV made a truce with Scotland, and his brother, the Duke of
Gloucester, later to be Richard III, was appointed Warden of the West
Marches. Yet the spirit of the Border remained alive, and the question of
the 'Debatable Land' on the border of the two kingdoms remained a burning issue.

63 *Plan of the upper
chamber of a pele tower.*

6

The Tudor Landscape

64 *Richard Redman, Abbot of Shap from 1458 until 1505.*

The first quarter of the 16th century seems to have been a period of rising prosperity within the two counties. Although short-lived, this increased wealth finds expression in a spate of monastic building activity, the final flowering before the icy winds of the Dissolution. At Shap, Abbot Richard Redman commissioned the impressive western tower which was probably built by the same masons who constructed similar towers at Fountains and Furness; at Carlisle the north-west gate of the abbey precinct was built in 1528, while at Holm Cultram in 1507 Abbot Robert Chamber added a magnificent porch to his monastery which, even in its much-altered present state, is a splendid testimony to late medieval architecture. But this St Martin's summer came to an end in 1536, for in that year Henry VIII's commissioners began their work of closing the monasteries, and among the first to go were Calder and Seaton. Although in the 16th century monasticism was no longer the potent force it had been in earlier centuries, nevertheless Henry VIII's threat to its very existence engendered the revolt known as the Pilgrimage of Grace. Essentially a rising against religious change, but also fired by a sharp increase in grain prices, the movement began in 1536 in Yorkshire under Robert Aske, a north-country lawyer, but soon men from Cumberland and Westmorland joined the 'pilgrimage' and representatives of families who had fought under the English flag at Flodden now marched under the banner of St Cuthbert. In north Westmorland Robert Thompson, vicar of Brough, gathered his followers around him and, joined men from Kirkby Stephen, they marched to Penrith. There they linked up with Sir Edward Musgrave and the men from Edenhall, and when the Greystoke contingent and the tenants from Holm Cultram arrived, the Pilgrims, now some 15,000 strong, marched on Carlisle. The city closed its gates to them and the rebels retreated to Cockermouth where they were joined by the Abbot of Holm Cultram. Meanwhile, on the other side of the Pennines, a truce between the Pilgrims and the Duke of Norfolk, the king's commander, had been agreed, and, reluctantly, the rebels returned to their homes. Popular discontent remained strong and in February 1537 a second rising began in Kirkby Stephen and Appleby and quickly spread to Penrith and Cockermouth; 6,000 insurgents gathered on Broadfield Moor, intending to attack Carlisle, but being leaderless they broke and ran before Sir Christopher Dacre's forces. The king wreaked a characteristic vengeance and the bodies of 66 poor men, 45 from Westmorland and 21 from

Cumberland, were hung in chains in such villages as Mallerstang, Asby, King's Meaburn, Brough, Greystoke, Eaglesfield, Torpenhow, Branthwaite, Wythop, and elsewhere. The Pilgrimage of Grace had been crushed and the Reformation continued relentlessly; in 1537 Armathwaite was closed, and in the following year Holm Cultram, Wetheral, and St Bees met the same fate. Lanercost remained until 1538 and finally, in 1540, Shap and Carlisle Priory were dissolved.

The Dissolution of the monasteries—'the Northern Tragedy', as it has been called—has been portrayed as a social disaster for the northern counties and certainly there is some truth in this assertion. With the Dissolution went a valuable source of poor relief; for example, at an enquiry into the customs of Holm Cultram Abbey it was said that when tenants were obliged to perform boon days

> they had great commodity and benefit from them. For every plough for three days' work they received 17 white herrings and 6 red ones, ¼ of a killin (cod), ¼ of a salmon, 3 wheat loaves, 3 loaves of yeoman's bread and 3 gallons of ale, and at every harvest each person received for three days 3 loaves of bread, 6 white herrings, and 3 pints of ale besides that in the time of Christmas ... every tenant and his wife dines in the abbey, whereof ... since the dissolution they have been denied the said commodities.

65 *Sir Hugh Askew of Seaton. Knighted after the Battle of Pinkie in 1547, he died in 1562. Redrawn from the monumental brass in Bootle church, Cumberland.*

In addition, of course, the monasteries provided the only schools, and their closing dealt a severe blow to education. Their guest houses provided hospitality for travellers in this bleak northern area, and many people must have eagerly sought the welcome shelter of Shap Abbey as they journeyed over the windswept uplands between Kendal and Penrith; indeed, Shap fulfilled a very real need and this could be the main reason why the monastery was the last of all the Cumbrian houses to be dissolved.

For many monks and nuns, particularly the old and infirm, their expulsion into a harsh and seemingly hostile world must have come as a cruel blow, but to others it may well have been a welcome liberation. Those who wished to return to the world were provided with pensions which were not ungenerous; the last abbot of St Bees received £40 per year, a handsome sum, and in 1540 the 14 monks from Shap were granted pensions ranging from £4 to £6 per year, equal to about three-quarters of the average income per head before the Dissolution, while at Holm Cultram the awards ranged from £6 to £2 depending on length of service. Some heads of monasteries continued in their old homes, merely changing their titles; thus Lancelot Salkeld, the last prior of Carlisle, became its first dean, and Gawyn Borrodale, the last abbot of Holm Cultram, became its first rector; others like Thomas Aglionby, a former canon of Carlisle who became rector of Bewcastle, found new ecclesiastical posts within the area.

One of the economic consequences of the Dissolution was the redistribution of former monastic estates to secular ownership. The possessions of Carlisle and Wetheral were granted to the newly-established Dean and Chapter of Carlisle, while those of Holm Cultram were eventually given to Oxford University; the lands of Calder and St Bees were leased to Henry VIII's notorious commissioner, Dr. Leigh, while the extensive Borrowdale estate formerly owned by Fountains Abbey was sold by the

66   Among these 15th-century prisoners' carvings in one of the cells in the Great Tower of Carlisle Castle are representations of St George and the dragon, St Sebastian, the Crucifixion—and a mermaid.

Crown to Richard Greames of Eske in Netherby. Seaton Priory was granted to Hugh Askew, a minor court official, the manor and demesnes of Shap were leased to Thomas, Lord Wharton, and finally, after much political manipulation, Lord Dacre succeeded in acquiring Lanercost. It has often been argued that this redistribution of land resulted in hardship and a depressed economy; W.G. Collingwood has written that '... with the fall of the abbeys most of the industrial employment on which the dalesmen eked out a living, had been lost'. However, this does not mean that the economy of the two counties collapsed for, as the late Mary C. Fair observed, '... the sheep presumably went with the granges of the abbeys to the new grantees, and they would need shepherds, the bloomery hearths went on functioning and the charcoal business went on denuding the woodlands'.

Similarly, the bailiffs, journeymen, and other monastic servants probably found employment with the new owners. Nevertheless, the Dissolution resulted in a recasting of the economy; the monasteries had played an important rôle in establishing markets, and in some cases the monastic buildings provided a focus for a small urban community. After they were swept away, trade was routed through market towns; the wool from the High Furness fells was no longer sent to Furness Abbey but to the markets in Ulverston and Kendal; likewise, wool from the Fountains estate in Borrowdale found a market in Keswick and Kendal rather than in Yorkshire, and in the same way the markets of Cockermouth, Wigton, and Egremont increased their trade as a direct result of the closing of the monasteries.

Environmental limitations to farming have always dominated the agricultural scene in Cumberland and Westmorland; the high rainfall and corresponding high incidence of cloud shortened the growing season and this, together with a thin, acid soil dictated that the central fells should be concerned with the rearing of sheep, and on the coarse, hairy wool from these stony, windswept hillsides the prosperity of the Kendal woollen cloth industry was firmly based. The same environmental factors determined that oats should be the staple grain in these inhospitable uplands, and in the 16th century, as in previous centuries, haver bread, crisp, golden oatcake, was the main bread, and black oatmeal formed the basis of the diet.

In the lowland areas of West Cumberland, the Eden Valley, the Solway plain, and the Kent Valley, the lower rainfall and the increased sunshine figures, together with soils derived from boulder clays, afforded a more favourable environment for arable farming and in these areas barley and wheat were grown and cattle were reared. In these areas, too, there is abundant evidence for the existence of an open or common field system. It is almost impossible to say when this system of land management came into existence, but as far as the two counties are concerned the open fields appear to have been organised on an infield-outfield basis; that is, a tract of land near to the hamlet, the infield, was cropped every year, fertility being maintained by the application of manure, while the outfield was cultivated spasmodically and the land allowed to lie fallow for several years. Mr. Gordon Elliott's careful study of open fields in 16th-century Cumberland has clearly shown that this method of cultivation was widespread—out of a total of 288 townships in the county, 220 had open fields. Although the more fertile lowlands had the best-developed system of open field agriculture, recent research has indicated that several dales within the uplands had similar, though smaller, common fields. At

67 *A bird's-eye view of Elizabethan Carlisle.*

Wasdale Head at the end of the 16th century, seventeen or eighteen tenants had holdings in the 345-acre open field, but common grazings of the scattered fell farms extended over 6,000 acres. In Great Langdale there were two open fields, one at Middlefell Place, and the other at Mickle Ing, and there were other common fields at Nether Wasdale, Threlkeld, Mardale, Wet Sleddale, Greystoke, Penruddock and elsewhere. Indeed, it is true to say that open field farming in Cumberland and Westmorland reached its peak in the 16th century and with the rise of the yeoman farmer in the 17th century came a corresponding demand for improvement and enclosure.

There is nothing to suggest that there was any marked improvement in agricultural methods in the two counties during the Tudor period. Farm

68   *Arms of the Company of the Mines Royal.*

implements were heavy, crude, and cumbersome; the roughly-fashioned rowan-tree plough, drawn by four draught oxen, had no coulter or mould board and therefore merely scratched the surface. In the uplands, wheeled vehicles were unheard of, and goods were transported either on the backs of pack-horses or on clumsy wooden sleds. Sickles were used for harvesting grain with the result that a considerable quantity of stubble remained after harvest; this was used for thatching, and animals were allowed to graze the 'aftermath'. Threshing was done with a flail, an implement in use until the 20th century.

Stock management was unknown, since, in the absence of root crops, there was no means of keeping all the animals throughout the year. The great autumnal slaughter was the occasion for the preservation of meat either by pickling it in brine or by hanging it in the smoke of a peat fire. The most common breed of sheep was probably a cross between a small, black-faced indigenous variety and the Herdwick; each ewe seldom produced more than one lamb, and the coarse fleece weighed approximately three to four pounds. Flocks were small; Thomas Chambers of Raby Cote kept a flock of about fifty sheep in 1605, but the average number kept by Holm Cultram tenants was ten. Veterinary science was primitive, the most universal treatment for disease being a salve composed of tar, rancid butter, tallow and, in the 17th century, tobacco! Yet these thin, scraggy, ill-cared-for sheep best suited the harsh environment of the fells, and on them depended the well-being of the cloth industry.

Although the 16th century can hardly be considered as a period of agricultural advance, the last part of this century witnessed a remarkable development of mining activity within the Lakeland fells. Encouraged by Sir William Cecil's policy of fostering national defence and industry, the search for silver, gold and copper ores was intensified; accordingly, in 1564 the Company of the Mines Royal was founded by an agreement between Queen Elizabeth, Thomas Thurland, Master of the Savoy, and Daniel Hechstetter, representative of Haug, Langnauer and Company, the great Augsberg business partnership. The aim of the newly-formed business company was to 'search, dig, try, roast and melt all manner of mines and ores of gold, silver, copper and quicksilver' and the Crown was to have one tenth of all the gold and silver found. At this time German mining techniques were the most advanced in Europe so, in 1565, some forty or fifty 'Almaynes', German miners from such places as Schwartz in Styria and Gastein in the Tyrol, were brought to Cumberland to work in the new mines. The main mining centre was the Newlands valley near Keswick; here on the first day of April 1565 the Goldscope mine, thought to be a corruption of *Gottes Gab*, was opened, but the Germans were certainly not fools for this mine proved to be one of their richest workings. Other mines followed—Brandelgil on the side of Catbells, Stoneycroft near Stair, Ellers near Grange-in-Borrowdale, several workings in the Caldbeck Fells, north of Skiddaw, and at Threlkeld as well as smaller mines at Greenhead Gill near Grasmere, at Brigsteer and Whitbarrow near Kendal, above Thirlspot on the flanks of Helvellyn, and in the Buttermere valley. By 1600 the

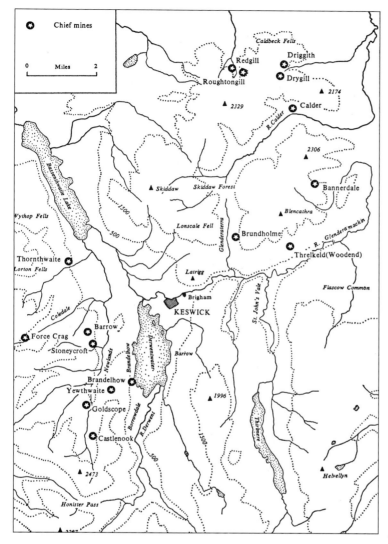

69 *The map indicates the main mines in the Keswick area; many of these workings produced both lead and copper ores. The Company had their main smelting plant at Brigham, to the east of Keswick. In addition to the mines shown here, the Mines Royal also exploited the rich copper ores of the Coniston area. Contours and heights shown in feet.*

70 *The Goldscope Mine in Newlands, Cumberland, thought by some to be a derivation of the German* Gottes Gab, *God's Gift, was opened by the Company of the Mines Royal on 1 April 1565—but these German miners were no fools, for this lead and copper mine proved to be one of the most productive workings in the Lake District.*

German miners had moved into north Lancashire and were exploiting the rich copper ores of the Tilberthwaite and Coniston fells.

The riches of the Lakeland hills were won by means of adits, horizontal tunnels, and shafts, and although the mining equipment consisted mainly of picks, hammers, and wedges, considerable quantities of copper, lead, and some silver ore were raised by the company during its activities in the north-west. Between 1564 and 1600 some £68,000 had been made by the sale of metal—but mining expenses were high and in the same period £104,000 had been spent on improving production. By the end of the 16th century the mines had adopted the most sophisticated techniques available for the raising of ore and the pumping of excess water; some indication of

the standard of mining engineering can be gained from a report made about 1600 by two surveyors who

> ... viewed the water engine newly erected in God's Gift and the course or stream that stirs the double wheel, which is brought along the side of the mountain almost 1,200 yards, in wooden troughs made of planks and from thence is carried through troughs within the mines, 26 fathoms, into a cistern of planks, from which it falls upon the wheels of the engine.

From the mines in Newlands, Caldbeck and elsewhere, the ore was transported by pack-horse trains to Brigham, near Keswick, where the furnaces, smelting houses and stamp mills were situated; by 1567, Brigham and Keswick had become one thriving industrial area with at least six furnaces in operation. Huge quantities of charcoal were needed to feed these furnaces and woodland was

71 *Mining ore, 16th century.*

purchased in many Cumberland dales; peat was used as a fuel and in 1571 no fewer than 53 men were engaged in carting peat from such areas as Skiddaw Forest, Wythop Moss, and Flaskow Common on the Helvellyn range. Without doubt, the Company of the Mines Royal considerably boosted the economy not only of the Keswick region but also of many other parts of the Lake counties; even as early as 1574 there was hardly a Lakeland dale which was not represented in the lists of people employed by the company either to work at Brigham or to cart peat, charcoal, wood and ore. By the beginning of the 17th century it was reported that '... about 500 persons dwelling near about the works are enriched by this means to the great benefit of the country'.

The expansion of the mining industry was not the sole success story in the 16th century, for the cloth industry also had its share of increasing prosperity. Although much of the wealth of the monastic houses in Cumberland and Westmorland had been derived from the sale of wool, it was not until the 16th and 17th centuries that the industries developed dramatically. Centred largely on the town and parish of Kendal with its 24 surrounding townships, cloth-making flourished here as a cottage industry because of certain advantages. Obviously the wool from local sheep was an important factor, but there were others; after the introduction of mechanical fulling in the 13th century, the fast-flowing becks of the Lakeland fells were harnessed to operate the wheels of fulling mills which sprang up in most of the dales, particularly in the 16th century. In 1453 the parish of

Grasmere, which included Rydal, Langdale, and Loughrigg, had six mills, but by the 16th century this number had been increased to eighteen. In addition, the dales possessed an abundance of agriculturally worthless land which could be used as tenter grounds where cloth could be stretched and bleached. Around the Kent valley, dyer's broom (*Genista tinctoria*) grew wild and cloth dyed with this was yellow in colour, but after re-dyeing in blue woad the distinctive and characteristic 'Kendal Green' was produced. Furthermore, a red dye could be made by processing mountain lichen and cloth dyed in this was much sought after. Two other factors deserve mention—first, the abundant soft water from the fellsides facilitated the dyeing of cloth, and second, the ubiquitous presence of green bracken which when burned provided

72 *Sorting and washing ore, 16th century.*

a ready supply of potash; this when mixed with tallow formed a crude but effective soap which was used to wash the wool. Research by Mr. M. Davies-Shiel has uncovered several hundred examples of the stone-built potash kilns in which the green bracken fronds were burned.

Not surprisingly, then, the cloth industry expanded so that by the 16th century trains of pack-horses clattered over the cobbled streets of Kendal carrying bales of cloth to distant markets such as York, Bristol, Southampton, and London. Indeed, Southampton seems to have been a market of some importance for the Kendal merchants and in 1552-3 the accounts of the Cloth Hall there contain the names of no fewer than 25 Kendal chapmen. Kendal cloth mistakenly acquired a reputation for coarseness; although coarse, hard-wearing clothes such as kersey and cogware were made and exported, and so, too, were fine cloths such as serge and baize. Falstaff in Shakespeare's *Henry IV* speaks of 'three misbegotten knaves in Kendal Green' but it should also be remembered that in 1543 Queen Catherine Parr, the last and arguably the most successful of Henry VIII's six wives, gave her husband a coat of cloth made in her native Kendal, suggesting that this was cloth fit for a king. Kendal no longer depends on its cloth industry as it did in the 16th and 17th centuries, but the town coat of arms bearing wool hooks and teazels still carries the assertion *pannus mihi panis*— wool is my bread.

73 *The first seal of the Corporation of Kendal.*

If the Tudor period was one of increasing affluence in Cumberland and Westmorland so, too, it was a period when settlement in the fells

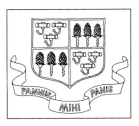

74 *'Wool is my Bread' —the arms of Kendal, showing teasels and wool hooks.*

expanded by the piecemeal carving out of small farms on the edge of the waste. At the same time many of the large 'forest' areas preserved as private hunting grounds were abandoned; by 1578 Copeland Forest had almost vanished, the northern section being reduced to a 'free chase' known as the Forests of Gatesgarth, while in the south the former hunting rights were restricted to Upper Ennerdale. Similarly, Tudor disafforestation in Inglewood meant that the central part of the Forest between the Petteril and the Caldew became open common grazing land, free from the restrictive forest laws. By the end of the 16th century the forests and chases, once the jealously and savagely guarded hunting preserves of lords and nobles, were transformed into huge common lands for the benefit of the tenants, a clear reflection that deer were being replaced by people.

If the building of chapels is taken as an index of increasing prosperity and population, then the 16th century features prominently in any inventory; Borrowdale chapel was first mentioned in 1505, Ennerdale in 1543, Wasdale Head *c*.1552, Wythburn in 1554, and chapels at Newlands, Mallerstang, and Mungrisdale occur for the first time on Christopher's Saxton's map of 1576. In 1557 Crosthwaite chapel near Kendal was consecrated and in 1571 Langdale and Long Sleddale chapels are first mentioned, and Witherslack is first recorded in an archbishop's visitation in 1578. In other cases chapels were made parochial; in 1562, the newly-built chapel at Troutbeck (Westmorland) was given parochial rights, and in 1580 the chapel at Matterdale was made parochial because the inhabitants claimed that:

> ... from the annoyances of snow and other foul weather in the winter season in that fellish part they be often very sore troubled with carrying the dead corpses ... and the infants there born unto burial or christening to their said parish church of Greystock.

But the building of these chapels was not the only sign of social change within the two counties, for a number of endowed grammar schools were opened: Kendal, 1525; Penrith, 1564; Kirkby Stephen, 1566; Keswick, 1571; Blencow, 1578; St Bees, 1583; Kirkby Lonsdale, 1591; Stainmore, 1594; and Dean, 1596; while the Grammar School at Appleby, which existed in medieval times, was refounded by Queen Elizabeth in 1574. These grammar schools performed a valuable service for they re-established the tradition of learning originally fostered by the monastic houses and in so doing compensated somewhat for the social deprivations which accompanied the Dissolution of the monasteries earlier in the century.

7

Town and Country in the 17th Century

The 17th century opened with a significant and far-reaching political event matched only by William Rufus's seizure of Carlisle in the 11th century for, in 1603, the Union of the Crowns brought not only a change in the political and social structure of the Border countries, but also a period of lasting peace and stability. No longer did fierce Scottish raiders threaten the economy and well-being of border areas; in their place in summer came droves of cattle from the Highlands and Southern Uplands moving to the markets of south-east England and bringing, incidentally, a measure of prosperity to towns on the drove roads such as Appleby, Brampton, and Penrith—all towns which once had good reason to fear the Scots. But even before the union of the two kingdoms the stirring of a social revolution of some magnitude was already being felt, for the second half of the 16th century and the first half of the 17th saw the emergence of a powerful rural middle class sometimes called the *statesmen*, but more accurately termed yeoman farmers. Although tenants of the lord of the manor, these yeomen farmers, because of their obligation to military service on the Border, enjoyed certain rights and privileges which, in effect, transformed their tenure into something akin to freehold. Theoretically, when the Crowns of England and Scotland were united, this border tenure was extinguished—at least that was the argument King James used in an attempt to reduce the status of the yeoman. However, the canny Cumbrians were a match for the 'wisest fool in Christendom' and they sought to preserve their jealously-guarded rights by litigation, but by the time the matter was about to be resolved, James was dead and the attempt to alter the ancient customs was abandoned.

In some ways the rise of the Cumbrian yeoman farmer can be traced back to the Dissolution of the monasteries; released from their obligations to monastic overlords, many families gained in wealth and status by the exchange and buying up of land. By means of such transactions, some yeoman families were able to transcend social barriers and pass into the gentry, but, by the same token, others seem to have lost their stake in the land, and these families descended the social ladder to become part of the labouring classes. On the whole, however, the power and wealth of the yeoman farmers increased dramatically during the 16th century—after all, this was a period of inflation when the price of wool multiplied five times between 1500 and 1600, but the fixed level of the yeoman farmer's customary rents guaranteed a healthy profit.

75 *Lakeland packhorse, from a painting in the Museum of Lakeland Life and Industry, Kendal.*

The period of peace and stability which resulted from the Union of the Crowns, coupled with the growing affluence of the yeoman farmers, brought about profound and lasting changes in landscape evolution. One of the most important involved the rebuilding of many of the farmhouses within the two counties; this 'Great Rebuilding in Stone', as Professor W.G. Hoskins has called it, was not merely a Cumbrian phenomenon—it occurred throughout England during the 70 years following 1570, but because of the remoteness and economic difficulties of the north-west, the innovations in building patterns were slow to arrive, and in Cumberland and Westmorland the 'building revolution' took place largely between 1650 and 1750. Before this period most of the smaller houses in this area were constructed around a series of carved timber cruck-trusses tied with a beam to form the shape of a letter 'A', and around the resulting framework, which looked rather like the upturned skeleton of a wooden ship, the house was built. It is not unreasonable to assume that this cruck-frame style of building had its origins in the pre-Conquest period and it certainly remained in use until the 17th century, when it was swept away to be replaced by the entirely new technique of load-bearing masonry. The sturdily-built, whitewashed, weather-beaten farmsteads, which are an inseparable part of the human landscape of the Lake Counties, are a direct result of this minor architectural revolution of the 17th century.

During the second half of the 17th century the pace of building quickened, and by this time, too, a standard pattern had emerged which Dr. R.W. Brunskill has called the 'statesman plan'. Although there are variations depending on the size of the house and the wealth of its builder, basically the new farmstead consisted of a single range of farm buildings and a dwelling house separated by a hallan, a cross passage which ran through the building from front to back, cutting the range into two. At the far end of the hallan opposite doors led to the kitchen or 'fire-house' and to the byre. The 'fire-house', so called because it contained the principal fireplace built into the cross-wall of the hallan, was further sub-divided by a wooden partition to form a bower and sometimes a buttery. Over the living quarters and the byre was an unceiled loft, open to the slates and rafters. Access was by means of a wooden ladder or, in superior dwellings, by a stone staircase, and in this room the children and the servants slept. This long-house plan, with men and animals living under the same roof-tree, probably had its origins in deep-seated folk traditions; certainly in the Crosby Garrett area, and no doubt elsewhere in the two counties, it was firmly believed that the smell from the cattle and other animals was healthy and an antidote against certain diseases!

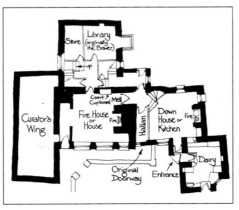

76 *Plan of Townend, Troutbeck, Westmorland.*

77 *Townend, Trout-beck, Westmorland. Built between 1623 and 1626 by George Browne for his wife Susannah, the house is an excellent example of a yeoman farmer's dwelling. It is a National Trust property and open to the public.*

One variation to the 'statesman plan', which became common in the late decades of the century, involved the separation of the byre and barn from the dwelling-house; the entrance to the living quarters was still by a hallan passage, but the doors led to a fire-house on one side and to a 'down-house' on the other. This room, often open to the rafters, was the service area of the farm where washing, baking, brewing and pickling was done, and here, too, the 'elding', the peat and wood fuel for the fire, was kept. There are many examples of this type of farmhouse within Cumberland and Westmorland and, although most of them have been considerably altered, traces of the original plan still survive. One of the finest is Townend at Troutbeck, near Windermere, built between 1623 and 1626 by George Browne, a prominent Troutbeck yeoman farmer, for his bride Susannah; the house remained the home of the Browne family until 1943. In spite of later additions, the down-house, the fire-house and the hallan, now a long narrow pantry, can all be traced, while the bower later became a library. The house is owned by the National Trust and is open to the public.

In the absence of documentary evidence, inscribed and dated stones built into the fabric of a farmhouse can be useful indicators, but they must be treated with some caution since it is not uncommon to find as many as three different date stones on one farm, relics of successive rebuildings. However, most of the date stones in Cumberland and Westmorland were carved between 1650 and 1750, emphasising the architectural importance of this hundred years. There are, of course, exceptions which prove the rule; the most magnificent of all the inscribed and dated stones in the two counties must surely be that at Hewthwaite Hall, near Cockermouth, which records that

78 *Circular iron girdle on which clap bread was baked.*

79 *The 17th-century barn at Townend, Trout-beck was built in 1666 by George and Ellinor Browne of Townend. Constructed on a steep slope, the entrance to the first floor, where the fodder for the animals was stored, was by a ramp or bank; the cattle were housed down below. It is possible that the north and south wings were originally intended to house farm labourers and that the gallery was used as a so-called 'spinning gallery'.*

John Swinbun esquire and Elisabeth his wyfe
did mak coste of this work in the dais of ther
lyf Ano Dom 1581 Ano Reg 23

In spite of what must be considered as improvements in housing conditions in the 17th century, general living conditions remained harsh. The basic diet consisted of meat which had been pickled in brine or hung in the open chimneys to dry in the smoke of a peat fire, and oatmeal in the form of poddish, or 'crowdy', made with oatmeal and the stock from boiling meat. In areas such as the West Cumberland plain, the Solway lowlands, and the Eden Valley, wheat could be successfully grown, but elsewhere the main bread grains were restricted to oats, barley and rye. Barley meal was used in the baking of a loaf of about 12 lbs. in weight and this would keep for four or five weeks in winter and two or three in summer; 'clap bread' or 'haver bread' made from oatmeal was baked on a circular iron plate or girdle and this would keep for considerable periods in the carved oak bread cupboards or court cupboards which formed an essential item of household furniture. That most careful observer of such matters, Celia Fiennes, saw clap bread baked in the Kendal area about 1695:

> They mix their flour with water so soft as to roll it in their hands into a ball—they have a board made round—this is to cast out the cake thinn—as thinn as a paper and still they clap it and drive it round, and then they have a plaite of iron—and so shove off the cake on it and so set it on coales and bake it.

Few green vegetables seem to have been eaten and the cheese made was largely skimmed milk cheese. In order to enliven an otherwise monotonous fare, spices were much used and most 'statesman' farms had a specially constructed spice cupboard set into the depth of the wall near to the fireplace, the warmest and driest place in the house. The oak doors of these cupboards, as well as those of the court cupboards, often bore the initials of the farmer and his wife, together with the date when the farm was built.

Self-sufficiency was the keystone of 17th-century rural life, and this was as true in clothing as in diet. 'Self-grey' or 'hodden grey' cloth, woven from the wool of black sheep and white sheep and therefore requiring no dyeing, was the most common cloth and 'harden' cloth, a very coarse material made from hemp and flax, was used for 'sarks' (shirts) and 'brats' (rough aprons). At night in the guttering light of a rushlight or the glow of a peat fire, men, women and children knitted stockings while stories were told, gossip retailed and folk legend passed orally from one generation to another. Wooden-soled clogs were universally worn by men

and women, rich and poor alike, for although they lacked elegance they were certainly practical, and warm in winter.

Medical practice was primitive in the extreme and most dalesmen relied on the hedgerow charms and cures which were handed down from father to son, from mother to daughter. Sometimes these were recorded in 17th-century commonplace books, and today make fascinating if somewhat gruesome reading. Many of these well-tried cures were to some extent medically effective, but others were superstitious nonsense—although it should be added that the power of psychosomatic medicine should not be discounted. Almost every community had a 'wise man' or a 'wise woman' whose advice was sought on medical matters; similarly 'bone setters', amateur osteopaths, were much called upon to set animal as well as human bones. In 1658 Sir Daniel Fleming of Rydal summoned the help of a number of local 'bone setters' when his son William broke his thigh, but unfortunately none of them was very effective and William was crippled for life. The fear of diseases was ever-present and epidemics took a dreadful toll; according to an inscription in Penrith church, pestilence killed 2,260 people in Penrith and 2,500 people in Kendal in 1597-8, though these figures probably include the surrounding areas. In the same period the pestilence raged in Carlisle, Keswick, Kirkoswald, Greystoke, Gosforth, Appleby, Kirkby Lonsdale and elsewhere. Again in 1623 there was a high mortality in West Cumberland, particularly in St Bees, and this seems to be a result of plague, and in the same year there was heavy mortality at Crosby Ravensworth. Infant mortality was very high, reflecting the standard of obstetrics and, similarly, the average age at death was low. In one or two areas there existed charities which assisted the needy elderly, but these were the exception rather than the rule; in 1653 that indomitable woman Lady Anne Clifford founded St Anne's Hospital in Appleby for the maintenance of 13 poor widows and in Kendal in 1659 Thomas Sandes, a manufacturer of 'cottons', provided almshouses for eight widows who were to work at carding and spinning. Lady Anne's hospital still stands on the east side of Boroughgate, and although Thomas Sandes's almshouses were rebuilt in 1852, the gateway fronting Highgate in Kendal still bears his arms and initials and the heraldic symbols of the Shearman Dyers' Company.

80 *The coat of arms on the gateway into the Sandes Hospital, Kendal. The initials are those of Thomas and Katherine Sandes, and the family arms are combined with the arms of the Shearman Dyers' Company.*

Despite the visitations of plagues and the general harsh living conditions within the two counties during the 17th century, there can be no doubt that the total population increased; although there are no accurate statistics, it is estimated that Cumberland and Westmorland may have contained between 54,000 and 55,000 people in 1600 and about 90,000 in 1700. Essentially rural in character, the population was scattered mainly in villages, hamlets, and isolated farmsteads at an average density of about forty persons per square mile; for example, Professor G.P. Jones calculated the density of population in Uldale in 1688 as 57 people per square mile; in Whicham, 38; in Lorton, 36; and 25 in Caldbeck. At the same time, however, the 17th century saw a period of commercial and urban expansion which gained momentum in the 18th century. At Ambleside the Countess of Pembroke obtained a market charter for the town in 1650 which secured not only a

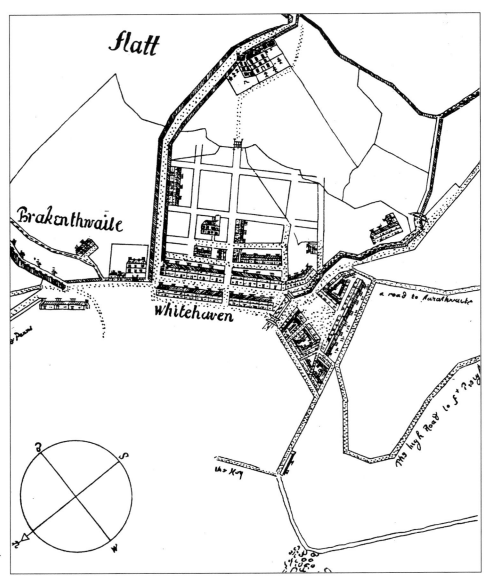

81 *A late 17th-century plan of the new town of Whitehaven.*

weekly market on Wednesdays, but also two fairs. Similarly, in 1687, Lord Wharton secured a market on Wednesdays for Shap, together with the right to hold three annual fairs, so replacing the amenities once provided by Shap Abbey before the Dissolution. It must be said that both these experiments in the creation of market towns were not crowned with success; Ambleside was unable to establish itself as a successful competitor to Kendal, and Shap's bleak situation amid thinly-populated moorlands was certainly one of the factors which precipitated a decline in the town's fortunes in the 18th century. Away on the West Cumberland coast, however, another exciting and more successful urban development took shape, for the new town at

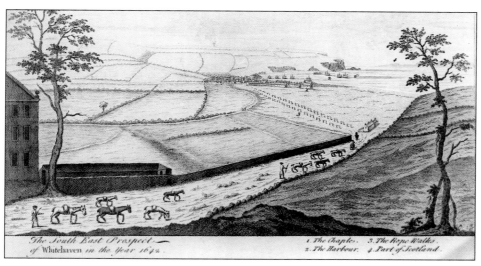

The South East Prospect — of Whitehaven in the Year 1642.
1. The Chaple. 3. The Rope Walks.
2. The Harbour. 4. Part of Scotland.

82 Whitehaven in 1642. Note the pack-horses in the foreground, the rope walk in the middle distance, and the ships sheltering in the lee of the pier built in 1634 by Sir Christopher Lowther.

Whitehaven was one of the wonders of the 17th century. Before the Dissolution, Whitehaven had been part of the properties of St Bees Priory, but later passed into the hands of the affluent Lowther family. Sir Christopher Lowther (1611-44) became lord of the manor of St Bees in 1630 and, recognising the potential of the small fishing village, built a pier at the southern end of the exposed bay in 1634. On Sir Christopher's death, his infant son John succeeded to the estate; when he came of age, Sir John continued his father's work by improving the harbour facilities and extending the coal trade with Ireland. In 1660 he secured confirmation of Whitehaven's right to hold a weekly market and an annual fair, originally granted in 1654. With an astute eye for the main chance, Sir John extended his estates and acquired the leases of coal-bearing lands which bordered his territories and, in 1678, gained all the rights to the foreshore between high and low water for two miles to the north of the town, thus effectively giving the Lowther family the sole right to load ships at the port. In 1685 the harbour, which until then had been under the administrative control of Carlisle, became a separate customs port with responsibilities for the coast between Ravenglass and Ellenfoot (later known as Maryport).

It was against this background, then, that the new town developed in the 1680s. From a population of about 250 in 1642, the town grew in size until at the end of the century it had over 3,000 inhabitants. The relatively easily-worked coalfields of West Cumberland meant that the pits around the town were producing almost 20,000 tons per year during the last decade of the century and, as the main market was Ireland, this stimulated the shipping industry. In 1676 the town had a fleet of 32 ships; in 1682, 40; in 1685, 46; and this figure was increased to 55 in 1689. Moreover in the 1670s a local sea captain had sailed for Virginia and brought back a cargo of tobacco, thereby initiating a trade which was to grow and flourish in the early decades of the 18th century. Meanwhile, in the years following 1680, the spacious rectangular grids of streets spread out over the meadows to

the north-east of the original village, and in 1693 the old chapel was demo-
lished and replaced by a larger one. By this time the success of the town
was assured, thanks mainly to the initiative and foresight of Sir John
Lowther. Sir Nikolaus Pevsner has called Whitehaven '... the earliest post-
medieval planned town in England', and so it is, but it is also arguably the
first planned town of the Industrial Revolution.

     One of the great figures in English cartography in the 17th century
was John Speed, a Cheshire merchant, tailor. Although his county maps
were based on original surveys undertaken by that other important cartographer, Christopher Saxton, Speed's most valuable contribution to map-
making was the introduction of detailed town plans as insets to his county
maps. His map of Cumberland, published in 1610, shows Carlisle with
commendable accuracy, and his Westmorland map shows not Appleby, the
county town, but Kendal. One of the most striking features of the plan of
Carlisle is that even in the early 17th century it was still a walled city,
apparently little altered since medieval times. Dominating the town is the
castle which had been repaired during Elizabeth's reign and her coat of
arms and the date 1577 may still be seen near to the massive keep, while
in the south the twin towers of the citadel, originally constructed in the
16th century as a second line of defence, control the southern entrance to
the city. The three principal gateways may be readily identified—in the
west the Caldew or Irish gate, in the east the Ricker or Scottish gate, and
in the south, the Botchard or English gate. The military nature of the city
is further emphasised by the fact that between the houses and the city walls

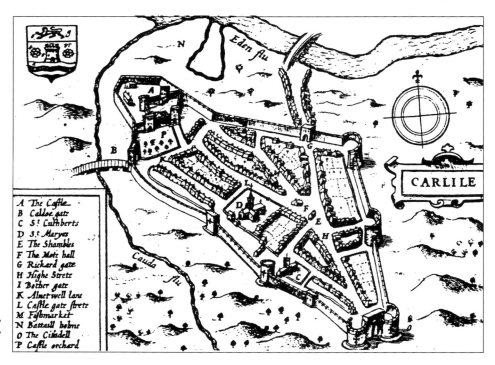

83 *Carlisle in the early
17th century. Map by
John Speed.*

there is an open space to facilitate the movement of troops to any part of the defences under attack. Indeed, one of the most striking features of the city is the area of open space and gardens, particularly in the vicinity of the cathedral and St Cuthbert's church as well as behind the houses in Rickergate. The Moot Hall and the market lie at the centre of the city with the butchers' shambles to the south-east and the fish market in the north-west. Although a precise figure for the population of Carlisle during the 17th century is not possible, a contemporary estimate suggests that there were about 2,000 inhabitants and 400 houses within the city walls, which were then 'indifferent strong and stately considering the time when they were built'. The map also emphasises the open nature of the countryside around the city; to the south-west the road to Wigton ran through open moorland and similarly the road to Dalston crossed Cummersdale Moor, while to the north of the city lay an almost impenetrable marshland traversed by a few trackways known chiefly to brigands and moss-troopers.

Thirty-four years after Speed published his plan of Carlisle, the city's defences were once again put to the test, for the town became the chief stronghold of the Royalists in the north. In October 1644, the loyal burghers found themselves once more besieged by Scots, this time under the command of George Lesley. The siege lasted for eight months during which time the citizens tenaciously held out, surviving on a diet of hempseed, dogs, rats, and any other edible material, and horses were kept alive by feeding them the thatch from roofs until that, too, ran out. Finally, on 25 June 1645, the city surrendered, bringing to an end one of the most harrowing yet at the same time illustrious periods in its long history. The price paid by Carlisle for its loyalty to the Crown was high; the suburbs had been burned or pulled down, the leper hospital of St Nicholas was destroyed, and by 1647 the city was 'a model of misery and desolation as the sword, famine and plague had left it'. By 1650, however, repair work was under way and stones from the cathedral nave and cloisters, which by then were in ruins, were used to repair damage done to the castle and the city walls. Within less than a century those same walls were once more fortified against the old adversary, the Scots, for in 1745 the city was besieged for the last time and the final chapter in the Anglo-Scottish hostilities was written.

In contrast to Carlisle's turbulent history, Kendal presents a more tranquil image. John Speed's plan (1610) shows a bustling, busy wool market and clothmaking town in the first phase of expansion. The urban layout of the town was dominated by the street running northwards from Nether Bridge and called Kirkland, Highgate, and Stricklandgate. At the point where Highgate passes into Stricklandgate and near to the market place another principal road, Stramongate, ran down to a second bridge across the Kent and on to the small suburb which was beginning to develop along Wildman's Gate. Unlike Carlisle, Kendal was not a walled town—the 'gate' element in the street names comes from the Old Norse 'gata', meaning a road or street—nevertheless, the town has two fortified sites and both are shown on Speed's map. The first and most obvious is the 13th-century castle perched high on its drumlin overlooking the town, though by the

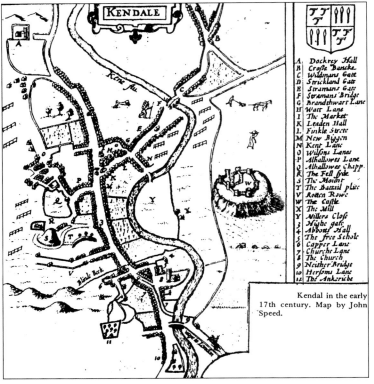

A. Dockrey Hall
B. Crofte Bancke
C. Wildmans Gate
D. Strickland Gate
E. Stramans Gate
F. Stramans Bridge
G. Brandthwart Lane
H. Watt Lane
I. The Market
K. Leaden Hall
L. Finkle Strete
M. New Biggin
N. Kent Lane
O. Wilfons Lanes
P. Alhallowes Lane
Q. Alhallowes chapp.
R. The Fell fyde
S. The Mount
T. The Battail plice
V. Rotten Rowe
W. The Castle
X. The Mill
Y. Millers Clofe
1. Highe gate
2. Abbouts Hall
3. The free Schole
4. Capper Lane
5. Churche Lane
6. The Church
7. Neither Bridge
8. Herfoms Lane
9. The Ankeriche

Kendal in the early 17th century. Map by John Speed.

84 *Kendal in the early 17th century. Map by John Speed.*

time Speed drew his plan it was already in decay. The second and more ancient fortified site lies on the western side of the Kent and is marked as 'The Mount'. Now known as Castle Howe and surmounted by an obelisk commemorating the 'Glorious Revolution' of 1688, this is the site of the 11th-century Norman motte and bailey castle of the de Lancasters. One other feature of the urban layout is conspicuous by its absence; there is no indication on Speed's plan of the famous Kendal 'yards' which run at right-angles to Highgate-Stricklandgate and Stramongate. It has often been argued that these long, narrow yards could easily be defended against Scottish incursions, but there is nothing to substantiate this colourful and romantic notion for, as Dr. J.D. Marshall has pointed out, the yards are for the most part a product of modern and not medieval history. In the 18th century, as the town expanded, the crofts and burgage plots behind the houses which flanked the main thoroughfares were built upon, so fossilising the ancient tenements and creating 'yards'. It should be added that this process was not confined to Kendal and can be seen in other towns in the north of England. Speed's plan contains one other feature worthy of note—on the steep fellsides and on the valley floor the tenter frames on which the famous Kendal cloth was stretched are clearly indicated, resembling, as William Camden observed, the Mediterranean vines. Like Carlisle, the population of Kendal at the end of the 17th century was approximately 2,000 but within a century this figure was to increase dramatically to 8,000 as the town entered its great era of expansion.

It might be argued that Carlisle, Kendal, and Whitehaven symbolise three important phases in the history of the two counties. Carlisle, the oft-besieged, battle-scarred, decayed, but tenacious fortress town representing the troubled period of medieval Anglo-Scottish border warfare, contrasting with the bustling, pushing market town of Kendal where the woollen cloth trade and commerce in general dominated the lives and livelihood of its townsfolk in the Tudor and Stuart periods. And away on the Cumberland coast Whitehaven, a planned and well-ordered seaport, grew apace, looking ahead to the new century, improved maritime trade, expanding industrial developments, and a new period of prosperity for the people of West Cumberland.

8

Mines and Mining

The industrial history of West Cumberland is inextricably linked with the development of coal mining for, in spite of formidable technical problems and its relatively small size, the Cumberland coalfield, extending some 14 miles from Whitehaven to Maryport, virtually monopolised the coal trade with Ireland in the 18th century. Yet even before the dramatic developments of the Industrial Revolution, the industry had made a small though not insignificant impact on the Cumbrian landscape; as early as the 13th century there were coal workings at Arrowthwaite, near St Bees, and at the end of the 16th century Sir Thomas Chaloner, lord of the manor of St Bees, leased areas of his lands to various individuals for the purpose of digging coal. Although other areas within the two counties—Caldbeck, Kaber, Hartley, Stainmore, and Barton—have a long tradition of coal mining, it was geology which dictated that the West Cumberland field should dominate, for here are the thickest and most productive seams.

At first, coal was exploited where the seams outcropped at the surface; 'day-holes' were opened and men dug the coal while women and girls transported it in baskets on their backs. In this fashion the 6ft.-thick Bannock seam was first worked commercially in the 1620s but soon the problem of drainage became acute; to drain the workings effectively it was necessary to draw off the water by means of an adit or horizontal shaft, but such work required the investment of considerable capital and this was provided by the Lowther family. The figure of Sir John Lowther (1642-1705) dominates the early development of the Cumberland coalfield; as well as overseeing the development of the town of Whitehaven, he revolutionised the methods of coal production, and after his death his younger son, James (1673-1755) carried on his father's work, so making the West Cumberland field one of the most technically advanced in Britain.

85 *Sir John Lowther.*

One of Sir John's early engineering feats was the development of the Howgill colliery and from 1663 vertical shafts of from 10 to 30 fathoms were sunk into the Bannock seam, the workings being drained by horizontal adits. The coal was winched to the surface by means of jackrolls or hand windlasses. At the beginning of the 18th century Sir John began to work the 9ft.-thick Main Band, but here the problems of drainage were considerable; the difficulty was overcome by the installation of a chain pump operated by a 'cog and rung' gin, the first time that water had been drawn off coal workings by engines. Further improvements came in 1675

75

86 *18th-century coal wagon running on wooden wagon way.*

when corves, circular baskets made of hazel rods, were introduced for the conveyance of coal; originally having a capacity of 2° cwts., the corves gradually increased in size as pits became larger and horse-gins superseded the primitive jackrolls. In 1682 attempts were made to improve the transport network and proposals were advanced for the construction of a 'coalway' or 'causeway' bordered on each side by timber baulks on which the carts should run. The proposal was put into effect in the following year and subsequently this revolutionised not only the method of moving coal but the whole transport scene, for in this simple but effective idea lay the seeds of railway communication.

Such developments served to increase the output of coal and the wealth of the Lowther family; in 1695 the Howgill colliery produced 15,196 tons of coal and the older Greenbank colliery contributed a further 2,231 tons. However, Sir John was not the only influential landowner interested in the exploitation of coal; on their Moresby estate, north of Whitehaven, the Fletcher family began to work coal. Fearing competition, Sir John at first successfully thwarted the Fletchers' plans to develop Parton as a port by claiming that he had been given land below high and low water marks by the Crown in 1678, but by 1705 the Lowther opposition had been overcome, a pier was built at Parton and soon Moresby coal entered into keen competition with Whitehaven coal on the Dublin market. Further north in the Workington area the Curwen family played out the same rôle as the Lowthers at Whitehaven and encouraged the exploitation of the coalfield by the injection of capital and expertise. In spite of drainage problems, by the 1740s four pits had been sunk south of Workington and by the end of the century the principal colliery at Chapel Hill was working the productive Main Band seam near to the coast. A few miles further along the coast the Senhouse family attempted to exploit the coalfield in the Ellen Valley area, but their efforts were not entirely successful. However, their endeavours in another direction were more fruitful, and in 1749 Humphrey Senhouse, junior, created a new town at the mouth of the river Ellen; clearly influenced by the planning of Whitehaven by the Lowthers, he adopted a grid-iron pattern of streets and christened his new urban creation Maryport in honour of his wife. In 1754 an iron works was built north of the harbour and the success of the port further stimulated the exploitation of the coal seams in this northern part of the field so that by 1780 there were collieries at Ellenborough, Dearham, and Birkby.

Undoubtedly, then, the period between 1650 and 1750 saw a tremendous increase in coal output from the Cumberland field, but the bald statistics give no indication of either the conditions in the mines or the hardships and privations suffered by the miners. With the increase in the depth of the mines, so, too, the hazards of mining increased; horse gins drew up the shafts not only the corves of coal but also the colliers, the more imprudent miners often riding the shaft simply by thrusting a leg through a loop in the winding rope, or by clinging to the rope with hands and feet. Needless to say, fatal accidents were commonplace. The presence

of methane gas and water presented other problems which had to be surmounted before production could be increased, and the Lowthers were
especially fortunate in that they had the services of a remarkable family,
the Speddings. In 1685, Edward Spedding became chief steward of the
Lowther estates at Whitehaven, and his eldest son, John, who succeeded
him, was responsible for the installation in 1716 of a Newcomen atmospheric
pumping engine at Stone pit. By means of this engine, the first of its kind
in the north-west, it was possible to drain the pit much more efficiently and
so make possible mining at greater depths.

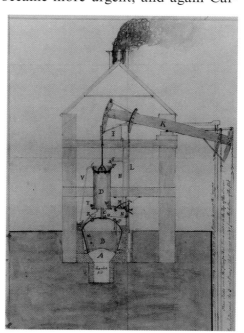

87 *Carlisle Spedding's 'steel mill', 1730.*

It was John Spedding's younger brother, Carlisle, who first attempted
to solve the problem of methane gas explosions which annually claimed
their toll of human lives. In 1730 he developed a 'steel mill' as a means of
illumination which, he believed, would not ignite the gas; this consisted
basically of a series of hand-cranked geared wheels which turned a steel
disc against which a piece of flint was held, thus giving off a stream of
sparks sufficient to give a dim light. Such 'steel mills' were usually operated
by a small boy who worked by the side of the collier. Primitive though it
was, Spedding's invention was somewhat safer than a naked candle and in
those pits plagued by gas the sparks provided better light than the alterna-
tive form of illumination, stinking pieces of phosphorescent putrefying fish
or fragments of phosphorescent wood. A measure of the success of the
'steel mill' may be gained by the fact that within a few years the device had
been adopted by most of the coal pits in the north of England and it was
used until the invention of the Davy lamp in 1819. As the pits increased in
depth so the problem of ventilation became more urgent, and again Carlisle Spedding found a partial solu-
tion; he introduced a system of
'coursing the air' which involved the
direction of air currents down certain
shafts and, by a series of ventilation
doors, re-directing them up other
shafts. Like the 'steel mill', this was
a simple but at the same time significant development which, by improving working conditions, also
increased output.

The culmination of Spedding's
work was the sinking of the Saltom
pit on the coast, close to the high
water mark. Work commenced in
1730 and was completed by 1731.
This pit was undoubtedly the most
remarkable coal mine of its day, not
only because of its unprecedented
depth of 456ft. but because it was
the first to commence the mining of

88 *The Ginns 'fire engine', Whitehaven, Cumberland. A New-comen 'fire engine' or steam pumping engine, was installed at the Ginns in Whitehaven c.1716. The introduction of such pumps made it possible to increase the depth of the mines and so increase the output of coal.*

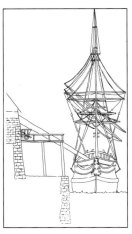

89 *Diagram of a coal 'hurry' at Whitehaven, c.1745, showing the method of loading coal into ships.*

coal beneath the Irish Sea. The workings were drained by a new and improved Newcomen atmospheric pumping engine and, without this extensive undersea mining would not have been possible. Such an audacious undertaking was regarded with astonishment; it was not only the colliery which excited approbation, for the method of transporting the coal to the harbour was an object of wonderment; although 'coalways' had been developed in the 17th century, Spedding's wagonway was much more ambitious. Sir John Clerk, one of the many visitors to the mines, has left an account of the transport arrangements in 1739:

> The coal ships are loaded by a contrivance of 3 stories of timber spouts which receive the coal from the height where it is brought by low wagons which hold 2 chalders (about 5 tons). These wagons run upon 4 little cast iron wheels on a cassey way [causeway] declining easily bordered by oaken planks or trees ... [and are] drawn by one horse only because of the gentle declivity of the caseways.

Such efficient handling of the coal at the surface, together with improved mining techniques below ground, clearly made the Saltom pit one of the most outstanding feats of mining engineering in the country, and coal continued to be worked in the mine until 1848. Carlisle Spedding lost his life in a mining accident in 1755, but his work was continued by his son, James, who sank several new pits, the most important being the Croft pit which was worked from 1774 until 1903.

Although much is known of the early mining techniques employed in the Cumberland coalfield, sadly, not much is known of the conditions of the miners, though it requires little imagination to appreciate the dangers to life and limb. The Speddings had certainly improved the conditions underground, but unfortunately explosions and roof falls remained common. The list makes dismal and depressing reading—in 1682 a violent explosion at Priestgill pit near Hensingham killed one man and injured six others; in 1737, another gas explosion at Corporal pit, Arrowthwaite, killed 21 men, one woman, and three horses, while at Hinde pit three years later two people were killed in an explosion which resulted in considerable damage and the closing of the pit for several weeks. In 1791 an accident of a different kind occurred when a vast quantity of water burst into the workings below Whitehaven, drowning two men, one woman, and five horses, and resulting in subsidence and damage to property on the surface. In the early 19th century the toll of lives increased; in 1819 at Kells pit in the Howgill colliery, 20 people were killed, and in 1821, at William pit, one of the most accident-prone in Cumberland, five 'haggers' (hewers), and seven boys and girls lost their lives in an explosion, and this in turn was followed two years later by a disaster in which 15 men, 15 boys, two girls and 17 horses were killed. In July 1837, 27 people and 28 horses were killed when the sea broke into J.C. Curwen's Chapel Bank colliery at Workington, the only occasion when the sea has inundated a Cumberland mine.

At the beginning of the 19th century the working day was between eight and nine hours and hours and wages varied according to the job undertaken; the earnings of 'haggers' (hewers) varied with output and also

with the coal seam in which they worked, but it is estimated that an average hagger could earn from 21 shillings to 24 shillings per week and the
best could earn 35 shillings. Other highly paid workers were the blasters
who received £1 per week, and the waggoners with approximately £1 1s.
0d. per week, while the lowest paid were the gin drivers, changers, gate
watchers, and slate pickers who earned between four shillings and 1s. 9d.
per week. Low as these wages appear, it must be said that they were higher
than wages paid to farm labourers and it seems that, in spite of the attend-
ant dangers, coal mining drew men from agriculture into the pits. Of the
453 employees at Howgill colliery in 1802, 124 were women; the youngest
workers were Joseph Toppin, a slatepicker (2s. 6d. per week) and Jane
Atkinson, a tracer (5s. 6d. per week), both nine years old, and the oldest
was Richard Kirkbride, 89, who worked above ground for four shillings
per week. At John Christian Curwen's Workington collieries—and doubt-
less in other pits, too—it was not uncommon for five-year-old children to
be employed to carry lights for miners for as long as 13 hours per day. In
1804, James Wilkinson, a boy of seven, was bound apprentice in Curwen's
mines for 14 years as a coal-hewer and engine-man; acknowledging his
tender years, the indenture concedes that

> ... in the meantime, and until the said Apprentice is of fit Age and Strength to be
> employed in the aforesaid business; He is to be employed in attending Trap doors,
> Cleaning of Roads, Drawing of Horses under ground, or any other offices, in any of
> the Coal Works of his said Master, and the said Apprentice shall and will find and
> provide for himself, Meat, Drink, Washing and Lodging and also all proper and
> necessary Wearing Apparel during the said Term of fourteen years.

90 *Women working in
a coal mine.*

For working long hours alone in darkness and discomfort, young James
received five shillings per week for his first four years, six shillings for the
next four years, seven shillings for the following three years, and finally
eight shillings for the last three years of his apprenticeship.

Writing of the William pit in the early decades of the 19th century,
one observer was moved to record his pity for

> ... a number of children who attend at the doors to open them when the horses pass
> through, and who in this duty are compelled to linger through their lives, in silence,
> solitude, and darkness, for sixpence a day. When I first came to one of these doors,
> I saw it open without perceiving by what means, till, looking behind it, I beheld a
> miserable little wretch standing without a light, silent and motionless, and resembling
> in the abjectness of its condition some reptile peculiar to the place rather than a
> human creature ... Few of the children thus inhumanly sacrificed were more than
> eight years old, and several were considerably less, and had barely strength to
> perform the office that was required of them ... Surely the savages who murder the
> children which they cannot support are merciful compared with those who devote
> them to a life like this.

Conditions in West Cumberland's coal mines were clearly horrific in the
18th and early 19th centuries, but in the lead mines of East Cumberland
they were greatly superior, largely because of the enlightened attitude of
the mine owners, the London Lead Company, a Quaker organisation
founded by Royal Charter in 1692. Lead mining in the Alston Moor area
of the northern Pennines has an ancient history—there are grounds for

believing that the Romans worked and smelted lead in this area and, certainly from the 12th century, lead and silver were exploited in the upper reaches of the South Tyne Valley in the Garrigill area. But the great period of expansion came after 1706 when the London Lead Company acquired some mines on Flinty Fell between the South Tyne and the river Nent; later, the company expanded its interests by leasing from Greenwich Hospital the former estates of the executed Earl of Derwentwater which he had lost to the Crown following his involvement in the disastrous 1715 Jacobite rebellion. By 1745 the company had become the most important mining concern in this remote part of Cumberland, and in that year they bought the recently-constructed Nenthead smelt mill and, following the discovery of the rich Rampsgill vein, the upper Nent Valley developed as a small enclave of industrialisation in a rural setting.

Before the arrival of the London Lead Company, little attention had been given to the welfare of the miners; many lived in Alston and walked each day to work, while others lodged in nearby farms or simply inhabited crude turf-built, thatched huts near to the mine entrances. Such conditions troubled the Quaker-controlled company and in 1753 they began the construction of a true mining village alongside the mines at Nenthead, one of the earliest 'company settlements' in the north-west. Moreover, the company encouraged miners to develop interests in farming, probably as a safeguard against lean times, and most of the cottages built by the company had about six acres of land which could be worked as a smallholding as well as 50 acres of bleak, acid, unenclosed fellside for grazing. The duality of mining and farming succeeded, and the London Lead Company brought prosperity to this inhospitable corner of the Pennines; a measure of this prosperity can be gauged by the fact that in 1767 there were 121 mines producing ore worth £77,162.

Much of the profit made by the Company was used to improve mining techniques; in 1769 wagon ways with cast-iron rails were introduced into the mines, and early in the 19th century lead pipes were used to improve ventilation. However, the major engineering achievement was unquestionably the building of an underground level or *sough* to drain the mines in the Nent Valley and to allow deeper working. Costing over £81,000, the Nent Force Level ran underground from the mines at Nenthead to Alston, some 4˜ miles away; work was begun in June 1776, but the entire operation was not completed until 1842. In the event, the level not only served as a drain, it also acted for a time as an underground canal along which 30-foot barges carried spoil. During the early 19th century the fame of this underground waterway was such that it became a tourist attraction and boat-loads of elegant 'tourists' braved the mock-perils of a candlelit journey from Alston to view a subterranean waterfall. Today all indications of the entrance have vanished but deep underground the Nent Force Level still exists.

The mining of coal and lead clearly rewarded those who had capital to invest and the fortunes of the Lowthers, the Curwens and the Senhouses were greatly increased by the expansion of these mines. However, hidden

VIII *Bridge End Farm, Little Langdale. This 17th-century farm is typical of the period known as 'The Great Rebuilding in Stone', when the old timber-framed farm houses were pulled down and rebuilt again in stone. Here the byre and the farm are under the same roof, perhaps reflecting the strongly-held belief that the smell of animals helped to keep disease away. The house is weatherproofed by a layer of white lime rendering but the byre needs no such protection. Until 1974 the farm lay just within the Lancashire county boundary.*

IX *The magnificent date stone over the door of Hewthwaite Hall, near Cockermouth, reflects the confidence of the builders, John and Elizabeth Swinbu(r)n. The house was completed in 1581 in the 23rd year of Elizabeth I's reign.*

X *Whitehaven 1735. Within less than a century, the town was transformed from a small port into the earliest post-medieval planned town in England. Its wealth was based on the export of coal from the nearby mines to Ireland, and the import of tobacco from Virginia. Painting by Matthias Read.*

XI *A Herdwick tup (ram) painted by a Westmorland artist, W. Taylor Longmire (1841-1914). Herdwicks were much prized for their ability to withstand the harsh conditions of the fells and they still form a significant part of fell flocks.*

away in the Borrowdale Fells was another mining enterprise which, if it could not rival the extent of coal and lead mines, certainly achieved a widespread reputation. Black lead, 'wad', graphite or plumbago had been worked on the hillside above Seathwaite certainly since the 16th century and possibly even earlier; a form of carbon occurring in 'pipes' in the rock, it was used locally by shepherds to mark their sheep. By the 18th century the versatility of graphite had been realised, and soon it was a much-sought-after and highly valued commodity used in the casting of bomb-shells, round-shot, and cannon balls, the glazing of pottery, the fixing of blue dyes, the prevention of rusting, and the manufacture of lead pencils. Powdered graphite was even used as a medicine to cure stomach ailments!

Obviously such a useful product commanded a high price on the open market, so much so that graphite entered into the smuggling trade and miners were searched before they left work in an attempt to reduce pilfering, for a pocketful of 'wad' was as good as a day's wage. On one occasion in 1751 armed men made an attack on the offices of the mine superintendent but, in true Wild-West style, they were driven off with musket fire! The following year an Act of Parliament made the stealing or receiving of graphite a felony and the culprit liable to imprisonment with hard labour. Yet with graphite fetching £3,300 a ton in 1788 it is unlikely that even these dire penalties entirely eradicated smuggling. By the 19th century the fate of all mining activities began to overtake the Seathwaite mine—the deposits gradually became exhausted; although early in the century several new 'pipes' were discovered, by the 1830s the output declined, and in 1836 it was reported that 12 men had been regularly employed in the mines for 15 months '... without so much as falling in with even a single sop of the valuable material'. The mine was worked intermittently until the 1880s, but the great days were over. Down in Keswick, the Cumberland Pencil Company, a direct result of the plumbago deposit, still manufactures pencils, though using only imported materials.

91 *During the 18th century, the port of Whitehaven emerged as a serious rival to Bristol and Liverpool. Under the influence of the Lowther family, Whitehaven grew from being one of the earliest post-medieval planned towns in England to one of the largest towns in the north of England by 1816. The grid-iron plan and the elegant Georgian architecture and graceful porticoes reflect this great age of prosperity.*

9

The Last Invasions—the '15 and the '45

On a November day in 1688, Edward Stanley, of Dalegarth, then High Sheriff of Cumberland, proclaimed the accession of William III at Carlisle Cross. Already some members of prominent families, including Sir John Lowther, had overtly pledged their loyalty to the Prince of Orange, but other adhered firmly to the old faith and remained equally firm in their allegiance to the Jacobite cause; among them were the Howards of Corby, the Warwicks of Warwick Hall, the Dacres of Lanercost, and the Stricklands of Sizergh, whose unwavering support for the House of Stuart drove them into exile with James II. When, in 1715, the Highlands rose in support of the Old Pretender, the heads of several of these families soon found themselves behind bars in Carlisle Castle, but on the whole the Jacobite cause failed to arouse much local support. On 15 October 1715, the good Bishop William Nicolson issued a pastoral letter to all his clergy in the Carlisle diocese exhorting them to 'animate and encourage your respective parishioners in the defence of their Religion, Laws, and Liberties', but a fortnight later the Highlanders were at Longtown, merely a short distance from the city walls. Although the garrison at Carlisle was far from strong, the rebels decided to avoid the city and turned instead to Brampton where they proclaimed James Stuart as king, under the title of James III. By this time, the local militia, armed with scythes, pitchforks, billhooks, and obsolete Civil War muskets, assembled on Penrith Fell to meet the invaders; led by Lord Lonsdale and Bishop Nicolson, who arrived on the field in his coach-and-six, the untrained Cumbrians were no match for the Highlanders and soon they fled. Lord Lonsdale, too, galloped off to Lowther Hall, leaving the Bishop in a dilemma; his coachman, however, deciding that discretion was the better part of valour, whipped up the horses and carried his reverend and gallant master back home to Rose Castle. Legend says that the Bishop,

92 *Lord Lonsdale's letter to Mr. Rowlandson 'about ye Rebells in Scotland and Northumberland' dated 16 October 1715. Thomas Rowlandson of Kendal was 'Treasurer of monies raised in Westmorland by virtue of several statutes made concerning the militia'.*

while shouting from the carriage window to his coachman to stop, lost his episcopal wig! The incident was later commemorated in verse by a local poet, Thomas Sanderson:

> The Bishop gain'd his snug retreat
> Thank'd Heaven he breath'd the air;
> And all his bliss had been complete,
> Had not his head been bare.
> For, ah! when on a length of road
> His troubles waxed great,
> The thatch, which hat and wig bestow'd,
> Unkindly left his pate!

As for the Jacobites, they marched unopposed into Penrith, where once again they proclaimed King James III, and then on by way of Appleby, Kendal, and Lancaster to Preston, where, on 14 November, they surrendered to General Willis. Many of the captured rebels were tried in Carlisle in November 1716; 25 prisoners pleaded guilty and were sentenced to death, but were not executed, and 26 more were discharged. Of the local families who joined the rebellion, James Radcliffe, the last Earl of Derwentwater, was executed on Tower Hill and his lands confiscated by the Crown and passed, ultimately, to Greenwich Hospital, while John Layburne of Cunswick managed to save his life but lost his estates.

93 *Charles Edward Stuart, the Young Pretender.*

If aspects of the '15 rebellion have a faintly comic air, the '45 invasion was altogether a more serious matter. On 25 July 1745, Prince Charles Edward Stuart, grandson of James II, landed on the mainland of Scotland; by 17 September he had occupied Edinburgh and by 9 November had arrived at Moorhouse within a mile or so of Carlisle. As was the case 30 years before, the city's defences were in a lamentable state; the garrison consisted of 80 soldiers described as 'very old and infirm' aided by seven companies of militia consisting of 287 men from Cumberland and 249 from Westmorland, hardly any of whom were properly equipped. Colonel Durand was in command of the garrison but was considerably incapacitated by gout; he had requested the assistance of 500 men, due from Ireland, but was informed that 'Carlisle was not, nor could be, of consequence enough to put the Government to the charge of sending an express on purpose'; neither could General Wade in Newcastle help the beleaguered city since the road between Newcastle and Carlisle had fallen into disrepair and was virtually impassable. So Carlisle waited and watched—indeed, two of the local clergy were posted on the cathedral tower, armed with 'a large spying glass', to give advanced warning of the enemy's movements.

Sunday, 10 November, was a misty morning but, as the mist lifted about midday, the rebels were seen near to the city walls in the vicinity of all three gates. Panic spread through the town, but by nightfall the Jacobites had been withdrawn to join the main army encamped at Brampton and it seemed that Carlisle might again be by-passed by the rebels. But such was not to be; realising that no help was forthcoming from Wade, Prince Charles Edward bided his time. The two militia regiments in the city mutinied and withdrew, leaving the town defenceless, and on 16 November Carlisle sur-

94 *William, Duke of Cumberland.*

rendered. The mayor and corporation attended a ceremony at which King James III was proclaimed at Carlisle Cross and soon after, on bended knees, they presented the keys of their city to the Prince at Brampton. On 18 November and with impeccable stage-management, Prince Charles Edward Stuart, mounted on a white horse and preceded by 100 pipers in full Highland panoply, triumphantly entered Carlisle. The proud border city had fallen with little bloodshed and the gateway to England was open.

The capture of Carlisle gave the rebels a rare prize—guns, arms, military stores and 200 horses, but above all the prestige of victory and the encouragement to continue the invasion, for it no longer seemed a 'rash adventure'. On 22 November, the Prince marched south from Carlisle to Penrith where he made requisitions for 1,000 stones of hay and 10 loads of oats on Lowther Hall, Edenhall, Dalemain, Hutton John, Hutton Hall, and Greystoke Castle. All meekly submitted to the demand, apart from Lowther Hall, and in consequence the house was occupied by Jacobite troops for a short period. By this time the advance guard had crossed a snow-covered Shap Fell and arrived in Kendal where they halted until 24 November before proceeding to Lancaster, Preston and Derby. On the whole, the invading troops did little or no material damage during their advance, a reflection of the Prince's insistence on high standards of discipline; from the towns through which his army passed the Prince demanded arms, money, and provisions, but from private houses the Jacobites confiscated mainly pewter plates and dishes to be converted into bullets. The prudent had, of course, buried or hidden their valuables long before the rebels drew near; at Heversham, south of Kendal, the parish books record the expenditure of one shilling for hiding the communion plate—and the same books record the spending of five shillings for the ringing of the church bells when the rebels were defeated.

95 *A contemporary woodcut of the Duke of Cumberland and his army.*

On 4 December, Prince Charles entered Derby, so sparking off a run on the Bank of England; the Royal family prepared for flight to Hanover, and it is said the Crown jewels were crated ready for shipment, but the Jacobite council of war held the following day argued for retreat. By Saturday, 14 December, an advance guard of 100 hussars under the Duke of Perth had reached Kendal where they met with open hostility for by now the news of the retreat had spread throughout the two counties. Soon the pursuing English army led by the Duke of Cumberland was hot on the heels of the retreating rebels; in an attempt to capture the rebel artillery, the Duke advanced his troops over Brougham Common and through Lowther Park hoping to capture Eamont Bridge. The Highlanders were forced to turn and fight, first at Thrimby Hill and then at the village of Clifton where the rebels stood their ground behind the walls and hedges south of the village; eventually the Duke drove them from this position, but his men and horses were so exhausted that the was unable to follow up. The skirmish at Clifton was the last military battle ever to be fought on English soil; both the Duke and the Prince claimed it as a victory, not without justification—certainly the Highlanders had been ousted from Clifton, but they had succeeded in saving their artillery.

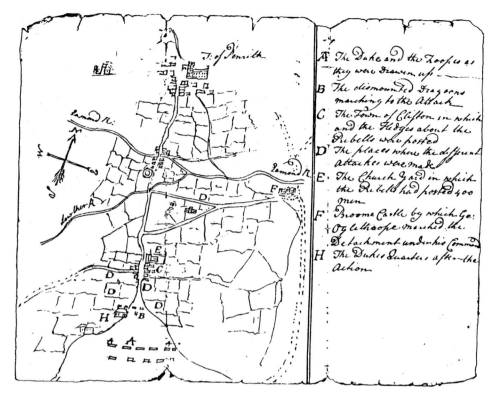

96 *A contemporary plan of the skirmish at Clifton, Westmorland, in December 1745. The Duke of Cumberland's forces are clearly indicated, and Penrith Church, Brougham Castle, and the rivers Eamont and Lowther are prominently shown. This was the last military battle to be fought on English soil, and both sides claimed it as a victory.*

On 19 December, Prince Charles entered Carlisle again, but this time a disappointed and dejected man for his cause was lost. Losing little time, he installed Colonel Townley of the Manchester Regiment as commander of the castle and its garrison of about 400 men, while Captain Hamilton was made Governor of the City. Mystery surrounds the reasons for his action—did he hope to re-group his forces north of the Border and once again advance on Carlisle to raise the siege which he must have known would follow his retirement? Or was it merely a last and desperate attempt to hold up the advancing English forces and so buy time for his retreating men? Almost as soon as Charles left Carlisle by the Scotch Gate, the Duke of Cumberland reached the city and at once made a detailed and careful survey. Derogatively dismissing the castle as 'an old hen coop', he went to Whitehaven for cannon with which to capture the city. In spite of Captain Hamilton's determined attempts to strengthen the walls with sand bags and the fixing of *chevaux-de-frise* to protect the gates, the city fell to the Duke's 18-pound guns on 29 December 1745, after a 10-day siege, the last in its long and turbulent history.

During the following months the rebel garrison and the town experienced the wrath of 'Butcher Cumberland'; on 10 January the members of the Jacobite garrison passed through the English Gate on their way to London and trial—many were to go to their deaths accompanied by all the barbarities which were then an integral part of the execution of traitors. In

97 *Carlisle after the rebels had surrendered to the Duke of Cumberland. The castle was contemptuously described by the Duke as 'an old hen coop'; it fell to his 18-pound guns and the Duke entered the city on 30 December 1745. The breaches in the wall can be clearly seen in this engraving.*

98 *Carlisle Castle, 1746. This engraving shows Scottish Jacobite prisoners being escorted to Gallows Hill, Harraby, for execution.*

Carlisle, many prisoners were housed in the cathedral under most insanitary conditions, and the subsequent outbreak of smallpox killed Jacobite and Hanoverian without discrimination. Troops were billeted haphazardly throughout the town, often without bedding, and food became scarce; moreover the situation was exacerbated after Culloden when more prisoners were crammed into the city's already overcrowded cells.

So many rebels awaited trial in Carlisle that the capacity of the judges and juries was exceeded and alternatives had to be found—between 300 and 400 prisoners were allowed to draw lots, and in this way one in every 20 was tried, and the rest transported overseas. Several of those condemned suffered their fate at Gallows Hill, Harraby, and others were executed at Penrith and Brampton, and the heads of the victims were impaled on the gates of the city as a warning to others; a traveller reported seeing these bleached and gruesome relics on both the English and Scotch gates in 1759 and some were still there, grinning from their poles, in 1766. The victor of the siege received his due recognition; a medal was struck to mark the fall of the rebel garrison which bears on the obverse the bust of the Duke in profile with the words 'William, Duke of Cumberland, British hero, born 15th April, 1721', while on the reverse appears an allegorical portrait of the Duke, clad in armour, dealing a death blow to a serpent representing 'Rebellion'. The inscription at the base reads 'Carlisle reduced and Rebels flew, December, 1745' and around the edge is the motto 'For my Father and Country', a sentiment which, ironically, could well have been voiced by another and perhaps less fortunate prince.

99 *The Duke of Cumberland's instructions to the gaoler of Appleby concerning the safe keeping of 63 Highland rebels and nine women. The document is dated 20 December 1745 and is signed and sealed by William himself.*

10

The New Agriculture

The so-called Agricultural Revolution had its origins in the more southerly and more fertile counties of England and, in comparison, Cumberland and Westmorland were backward, reflecting the isolation of the area and the difficult environment; indeed, a Cumberland contributor to the *Gentleman's Magazine* in 1766 was well acquainted with such hazards and dolefully chronicled the problems encountered in farming the fells:

> .. the middle of February is the middle of our winter and the farmers must have one half of their straw, and two thirds of their hay at that time, or their stock perishes. We cannot turn out our horses and cows to grass till the beginning of June ... add to this the winds and incessant rains, the latter end of the year, ... the land is kept so cold and spongy that we cannot sow oats before April, bigg [the substitute for barley] before June and the wet and frost in winter is very unfavourable for wheat, so that our lands, with the vast quantity of manure we must employ ... costs one third at least more to till than yours [in the south] do, and does not produce half the crops yours produces.

Dismal reading though this is, there is no doubt that there is much truth here, for the facts are largely substantiated by Arthur Young's reports on his travels in the two counties. In 1771 he claimed that the country between Keswick and Penrith was 'much of it moors and quite uncultivated, though evidently capable of it', while the area between Shap and Kendal he described as '... a continuous chain of mountainous moors, totally uncultivated'. Elsewhere his remarks are of a similar nature—the farmers 'know but little of clover', and 'cultivate some few turnips', while at Holme in South Westmorland he recognises a fertile, light loamy soil, but condemns the farmers for failing to employ a correct rotation 'and for this these slovens should be hanged'.

Similarly, farm implements were both few and primitive, being made almost entirely of wood, and even in the mid-18th century mechanisation was virtually unknown. Indeed, the plough, sickle, flail and ox-team so beautifully illustrated in the 14th-century Luttrell psalter were still in everyday use in 18th-century Cumberland and Westmorland. One of the things which never failed to surprise visiting agriculturalists was the relative absence from the Lake District of wheeled vehicles, and even in the 18th century the principal means of transporting goods was by pack-horse. James Clarke of Penrith, writing in 1787, made the possibly exaggerated claim that until the 1760s wheeled vehicles or carts were unknown in Borrowdale and comments that the farmers

... in carrying home their hay (for they make no stacks) ... lay it upon their horses in bundles one on each side; ... the traveller may even see hay carried in this manner through the streets of Keswick. Their manure they carried in the same manner, putting it in wicker baskets ...

100 *Ploughing scene in Eskdale, Cumberland in mid-18th century. The heavy wooden plough required two horses, two oxen and three men to work it. The painting is in oils on three wooden boards.*

Yet the very fact that Clarke felt it necessary to mention this at all could be taken to signify that by the end of the century this method of transport was an anomaly. The absence of wheeled vehicles in the central fells is perhaps not surprising when one reflects on the steepness of the slopes, and even today some farmers prefer the stability of the heavy wooden bracken sled to the convenience of the tractor. Outside the Lake District uplands, however, the single-horse two-wheeled cart was in use by the end of the 18th century; known as 'tummel cars', they were crudely constructed of wood with solid 'clog' wheels made of three pieces of wood fastened together with wooden pins and fixed to the axle which turned under the cart in suitable brackets. Such cumbersome carts had distinct disadvantages, not the least of which was the marked tendency for the cart body to part company from the axle and wheels. If carts were primitive, so was harness for the horses; 'braffins' or horse collars were usually home-made by plaiting hay and straw, bridles were made of cord, and halters of hemp or sometimes plaited rushes; only the most affluent yeoman farmers had leather saddles and 'sonks' or green sods, girthed onto the horse with hay bands, formed acceptable substitute saddles both for farmers, and for their wives and daughters.

Ploughs, too, were heavy and cumbersome and generally made from the wood of the rowan tree. Many 18th-century ploughwrights prided themselves on their ability to make a plough in a single day. Commendable though this undoubtedly was, the resulting plough can hardly have been an efficient implement, for it had no mould-board and could not turn a sod. Moreover, such heavy equipment required two horses and two oxen to operate it. The horses were harnessed one behind the other and the oxen yoked in pairs; one man drove the team, another held the plough beam down to prevent the ploughshare from slipping out of the ground, and a

101 *The breast plough. This illustration fails to convey the enormous physical effort necessary to use this most primitive of agricultural implements.*

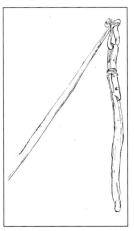

102 *A flail, a primitive implement used for threshing grain. Flails like this were still in use in the 1940s.*

third man guided the plough. When heavy, clay soil was being worked it was usual to include a fourth man in the plough team whose job it was to follow the plough breaking up the clods with a spade. Although not a plough in the accepted sense of the word, the so-called 'breast plough' was used in the 18th and 19th centuries to break new ground on steep fellsides. One of the most primitive implements in agriculture, it was similar to a long-shafted spade with a flange at right angles, which was pushed by the operator's chest or thighs; in difficult or stony ground an extra man was harnessed to the plough, like an animal, to add extra force. The turf was pared off, dried, burned and later forked into the ground so that a poor crop of oats could be coaxed from the most unpromising land. Not surprisingly, such heavy manual work has been described as 'the most slavish work in husbandry'. Other equipment was almost as primitive as the breast plough; although the scythe, or 'ley', was used in some areas, throughout most of Cumberland, and also in parts of Westmorland, the sickle was traditionally used for harvesting and, although back-breaking work, it was claimed by one writer that a girl in Cumberland could reap more corn in a day using a sickle than a labourer in the southern counties using a scythe. Similarly, crops were threshed with a flail as they had been for centuries and both the sickle and the flail were not ousted by the scythe and the threshing machines until the mid-19th century.

Within the two counties the range and type of agricultural equipment was clearly limited, even in the second half of the 18th century, but equally limited was the variety of crops grown. In 1794 it was reported that in Westmorland no pease, beans, clover or rye were grown and the following year Bailey and Culley, who surveyed Cumberland for the newly-formed Board of Agriculture, recorded that they saw only 'various patches of turnips ... at Netherby, Burgh, Dalston, and a few other places'. In fact, turnips were something of a curiosity and farmers would travel many miles to see an acre or two of this new-fangled crop! Although potatoes were introduced into the area rather late—according to one authority not until about 1730—they soon became a popular crop, and by the end of the 18th century they were providing food for humans as well as for pigs and cattle. Of the cereals, oats and barley continued to provide the bread for Cumbrians as they had for centuries; the damp, acid soils of the upland dales made the cultivation of wheat virtually impossible, but in certain more favoured areas, including the area of Ravenglass, in the vicinity of Carlisle, and on the limestone soils of south Westmorland, the production of wheat was feasible.

Until the second half of the 18th century the extensive fell lands of both counties remained unenclosed and consequently the chances of improving breeds of sheep and cattle were slender indeed. The most common breeds of cattle were Galloways and Longhorns, particularly on the Cumberland coastal plain between Whitehaven and Carlisle, and also in south Westmorland, while the main types of sheep appear to have been Herdwicks, which flourished best in the harsh upland environments, Blackface, and Silverdale. The wool from the first two breeds was coarse and full of 'kemps' or hairs and was sold for about 5d. to 5°d. per pound at the end of the century, whereas wool from the Silverdale breed was somewhat better and was worth about 8d. per pound.

Although there was no denying that until the middle of the 18th century the agriculture of Cumberland and Westmorland was backward, by the end of the century clear signs of improvement could be detected. James Drigg, a South Cumberland contributor to the *Gentleman's Magazine*, cheerfully announced that '... the things are now assuming a new appearance. The rust of poverty and ignorance is gradually wearing off ...'. Such changes were in no small part due to a number of pioneer agriculturalists. Of these men, Philip Howard of Corby Castle must rank high in importance for he was the first to introduce turnips and clover as field crops into the northwestern counties. In 1752 he had a field on his estate sown with clover to demonstrate the value of 'artificial' grass, and three years later he introduced turnips into the area, thereby improving the rotation of crops and providing winter feed for the animals. Prior to the introduction of root crops it was exceedingly difficult to find food for animals throughout the winter; in many areas of the two counties sheep were fed with hay, pease straw, corn straw, and even the leaves from ash trees. It was an offence under the orders of the Court Baron of the Manor of Windermere in the 17th century to 'cutt down or breake any other Men's Ash leaves', indicating that ash leaves were carefully harvested for winter food, and elsewhere there is evidence that sheep were hand-fed with holly leaves. Now, with the introduction of turnips and other root crops the great 'autumn slaughter' of animals, for so long an inexorable part of the cycle of agriculture, was not longer necessary. Moreover, for the first time, milk, butter and fresh meat, instead of the smoked and salted 'collops', became available all the year round and this in turn meant an improvement in the diet and standard of health of the inhabitants of the area.

Important though the work of Philip Howard was, his achievements were overshadowed by the pioneering efforts of John Christian Curwen (1756-1828). A friend of Arthur Young and acquainted with the leading figures in agricultural reform in England and Scotland, John Christian Curwen travelled widely at home and abroad, absorbing the techniques and technology of the 'new farming' and eventually bringing the fruits of his experience to his estates in West Cumberland and on Belle Isle, Windermere. Although his new ideas were enlightened they were not always entirely successful; his introduction of Devonshire cattle into the harsher environment of Cumberland was a costly mistake, and his experiments with imported merino sheep were not crowned with success; nevertheless, he succeeded in the breeding of shorthorn cattle and soon they became the most popular breed in Cumberland and Westmorland. It is, perhaps, an overworked cliché to describe Curwen as 'the father of Cumbrian farming' but it cannot be denied that his perception and enthusiasm laid the foundation of present-day Cumbrian agriculture.

103 *John Christian Curwen.*

Curwen's crusading zeal was carried well into the 19th century by one of his followers, Sir James Graham of Netherby in northern Cumberland.

Succeeding to the estate's 18,000 acres in 1824, he soon undertook the improvement of his land by draining it by means of the newly-invented tile drain. By 1849 some 12 million tiles were made and used on the estate, transforming what had been barren and poorly productive land into some of the driest and most profitable land in the country; '... where bogs and quagmires made it almost unsafe for humanity to tread ... the eye of the observer now rests upon large plots of arable land, rich in cereals, green crops, and pastures upon which first-class animals browse and fatten ...' ran one panegyric, without undue exaggeration. The lessons of tile drainage were not lost on another important landowner, for Lord Lonsdale soon established tile works at Lowther, Wetheriggs, and other places in northern Westmorland. Just as in northern Cumberland, so, too, on Shap Fell in Westmorland, the agricultural landscape was re-shaped and improved. Here, on the wild moorland between 1,200 ft. and 1,600 ft. above sea level, Lord Lonsdale concentrated his activities, first draining the wet portions by tile drains and then applying lime to neutralise the acidity in the soil, and eventually some 1,200 acres were drained and some 1,500 acres limed. Allied to the introduction of tile drains came the realisation of the importance of new manure like guano, nitrate of soda, and superphosphate, and by 1853 William Dickinson commented '... manures are now assuming the importance they are justly entitled to in rural affairs'.

During the early decades of the 19th century there were some remarkable changes in agricultural equipment. Slowly at first, but with

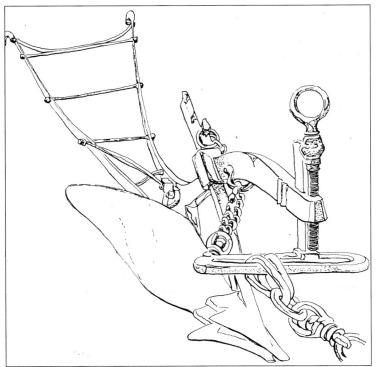

104 *A light iron plough, part of the Agricultural Revolution.*

quickening momentum, new techniques of farm-cart construction were introduced into the two counties; gone were the solid 'clog' wheels fixed to the axle turning under the cart, and in their place came the craftsmen-made dished wheels which turned *on* the axle, not with it. These single-horse carts helped to transform the agricultural scene at the beginning of the 19th century, making obsolete the pack-horse and the panniers; similarly, the work of the plough-team was revolutionised by the introduction of the light, iron plough. One of the earliest in Westmorland was brought from Scotland to Storrs Hall, Windermere, at the end of the 18th century by Colonel John Bolton; made by Wilkie of Glasgow, it soon superseded the heavy wooden implement then in use, and became a pattern for ploughwrights throughout the locality. By 1850, William Dickinson could record that 'they are ... re-markable for neatness of finish, and an absence of nick-nackery, and a simplicity and lightness of construction, with strength adapted for the stony soils of the county, and weighing from 12 to 13 stone each'. But their major advantage was their general manoeuvrability; no longer was it necessary to have a team of oxen and horses as well as three men to operate the plough—now it was the job of one man and two trusty Clydesdale horses. A revolution, indeed!

By the beginning of the 19th century, mechanical threshing had been introduced into the two counties; at first these new machines were greeted with suspicion, and, in some cases, hostility, but gradually they proved their worth, so that by mid-century there were 306 threshing machines in use in West Cumberland alone. Of these, seven were steam powered, one driven by wind, 71 by water, and the remainder by horse power. Drills for the sowing of grain, however, were adopted more slowly since the cost of these machines limited their use to the large farms, and even in the 1950s it was possible to see the broadcasting of seed by hand.

Of all the improvements introduced during the Agricultural Revolu-tion none had a greater impact on the landscape than the enclosure of the commons. Although enclosure of the wastes and also the combining of dales and strips into crofts and closes had been going on for centuries, after 1763 the movement accelerated dramatically; between that date and 1800 some 40,000 acres of common in Cumberland and 10,000 acres in Westmorland were enclosed and improved, and following the passing of the General Enclosure Act of 1801 the process was further stimulated. The impetus for this improvement of the waste land is not difficult to find; this was a period of increasing population and urbanisation and, moreover, between 1793 and 1815 Britain was involved in the Napoleonic Wars. Consequently, although there was an increased demand for farm produce, this could not be satisfied by importing from abroad and prices rose correspondingly, so encouraging farmers to reclaim the wastes and com-mons. Within the uplands of the two counties the fells were enmeshed in a network of dry-stone walls, stone boundaries which snake and dip over the steepest slopes, clinging to the mountain side as if they had not been built but rather had grown out of the fell like the rowan and blaeberries. Yet their ancient appearance belies their age, for most of these dry-stone walls were built during the early part of the last century.

Under the Act of 1801 the common rights were extinguished and the land re-apportioned among the promoters of the legislation and the holders of rights on the old commons. The cost of the new stone walls was to be borne by the recipient of the award and in several cases the award specifies the height and width; the award for Shap, dated 1813, indicates that certain areas are to be 'ring-fenced with a wall six feet high, thirty-six inches at the bottom and sixteen inches at the top'. Most enclosure awards specify a date when all the walls were to be completed and also who was responsible for the repair and upkeep of the new boundaries. For example, under the award for Wasdale Head, dated 30 June 1808,

105 *Wasdale Head from Westmorland Cairn, Great Gable. The pattern of the earlier, irregular enclosures on the valley floor contrasts with the more regular 18th- and early 19th-century 'intakes' of the fellsides.*

William Ritson his Heirs and Assigns to make and repair two fifth parts of the whole extent of the Fence up to Black Cragg beginning nearest the Inclosures and John Benson his Heirs and Assigns to make and repair the remaining three fifth parts thereof and so in the like Proportion to the Extremity of the boundary.

It is unlikely, however, that William Ritson or John Benson actually built the walls themselves, for most of these stone fences were constructed by bands of itinerant wallers who camped out on the fellsides for weeks on end, working from sunrise to sunset and coming down to the valley only on Saturdays. Conditions were harsh and wages pitifully low; writing of Westmorland in 1794, Andrew Pringle records that 'Seven yards and a half in length of a dry-stone wall five feet and a half in height, cost 1s. 6d. or 1s. 8d. building'. Although the wallers were skilled craftsmen, most of them were illiterate and unable to write their names, yet these men have most certainly left their indelible mark on the landscape of Cumberland and Westmorland.

By the mid-19th century the rural landscape had been transformed and had assumed a pattern which changed little during the next 100 years. The enclosure and improvement of the common land made possible improved agriculture, but not everyone benefited from such changes;

thousands of small farmers lost their rights of pasturage on the common land; many became mere farm labourers, others sank to pauperism, and, although it was not the sole cause, the enclosure movement certainly hastened the decline of the yeoman farmer. However, these things were not immediately apparent and a succession of writers greeted the new enclosures enthusiastically. Among them was James Clarke, the Penrith surveyor, who in his great *Survey of the Lakes* (1787) comments that

> ... cultivation of every kind has ... undergone a very great change within a few years; and ... though the harvest-cry, and the rural feasts and customs are still preserved, and though a boundary-stone is on some occasions still sacred, yet the number of hedges is mightily increased, and consequently the necessity of them in a great measure superseded: and I know not that there can be a more remarkable passage in the history of rural civilization, than the substitution of hedges in the place of the rude metes and boundaries so generally used in former times; and thus rendering the watchers of cattle needless, as well as giving beauty to the country itself.

If the 'watchers of cattle' were made redundant, there were, on the other hand, the fortunate ones who lined their pockets; to them the enclosure of the commons must have seemed like the final act in the transformation of a backward and retarded form of husbandry into an advanced and progressive agricultural economy. Indeed, it seemed that 'the rust of poverty and ignorance' had finally given way to enlightenment.

11

Turnpikes, Canals and Early Railways

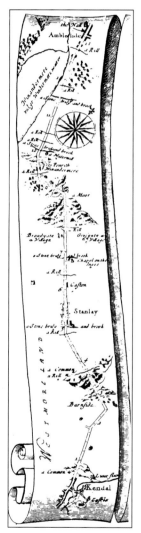

Until the second half of the 18th century, Cumberland and Westmorland enjoyed the unenviable reputation of having some of the poorest roads in the kingdom. Those travellers brave enough to risk life and limb came expecting the worst and were seldom disappointed. The mountainous character of much of the two counties clearly made travelling a hazardous and arduous business, and early writers were quick to point out the dangers. Typical of these reports is one left by three travellers who made the journey between Penrith and Kendal in 1634; this doleful account records how the intrepid adventurers went

> through such ways as we hope we never shall again, being no other but climbing and stony, nothing but bogs and myres ... on we went for Kendal, desiring much to be released of those difficult and dangerous ways, which for the space of eight miles travelling a slow marching pace we passed over nothing but a most confused mixture of rocks and bogs.

Forty-one years later John Ogilby's road book indicated only four roads within Cumberland and Westmorland: one from Kendal to Carlisle by Shap, a second one ran from Egremont, through Whitehaven and Workington by way of Cockermouth and Bothel to Carlisle, a third linked Cockermouth to Keswick, Ambleside and Kendal, and finally Ogilby recognised the Newcastle to Carlisle road which crossed the Eden at Corby and then ran eastwards through Castle Carrock. The indication of such roads, however, does not necessarily indicate that they were open for wheeled vehicles for it seems most likely that travelling was undertaken on horseback and goods transported on the backs of pack-horses, each animal carrying between two and three hundredweights.

However, the dramatic descriptions of early travellers in the northwest must not be allowed to obscure the fact that a communications network had been established by the end of the 17th century. Certainly in some parts of the two counties, travelling conditions were difficult, indeed, dangerous, but in other areas the pack-horse trains provided a reliable service. For example, the lead industry of the remote Alston area depended on pack-horses not only for the transport of ore to Newcastle, but also for the importing of foodstuffs from the Vale of Eden to feed the mining community. Certainly by 1750 the pack-horse traffic out of Kendal was well established, reflecting the town's importance as a flourishing textile centre as well as an expanding market town. By the 1770s, according to the historians Nicolson and Burn, this pack-horse trade had increased further

106 *Road from Kendal to Ambleside (John Ogilby's* Britannia, *1675).*

and it is believed that from Kendal alone some 254 pack-horses were entering and leaving the town every week, connecting this Westmorland town with such places as London, Wigan, Whitehaven, Cockermouth, Barnard Castle, Penrith, Settle, the Furness area, and York.

Clearly, then, the pack-horse system afforded a fairly extensive communications network, at least for the south Westmorland area, but the main disadvantage was its slowness—a journey from Kendal to London usually took up to 18 days, more if the weather and road conditions were poor. Moreover, the increased pack-horse traffic, not only in the Kendal area but in other centres, resulted in further deterioration of the existing road surfaces. Admittedly, the Kendal authorities were concerned about the state of the roads in the area and early in the 18th century surveys were made for Kendal Ward by Benjamin Browne of Troutbeck, the High Constable. In 1712 Browne concerned himself with the bridges in the Ward and noted that repairs were needed at Stramongate (Kendal), Bannisdale, Elterwater, Colwith, and Brathay. In 1730 he surveyed the roads only to discover that they were 'bad' or 'narrow', or 'covered with ye hedges'. The Garburn road, connecting Troutbeck with Kentmere, was said to be 'soe much out of repair and in decay, that a great part of it is not passable for either man or horse to travel through the said ways without danger of being bogged in moss or lamed among the stones'. Yet, despite Benjamin Browne's strictures, little was done to improve the situation until the second half of the 18th century.

As elsewhere in England, one of the most powerful influences in the improvement of road transport was the impact of the turnpike movement. The first Turnpike Act was passed as early as 1663 for the repair of highways in Hertford, Cambridge, and Huntingdon, and the Turnpike Trust was responsible for raising funds by levying a toll from the users of the roads. This simple but effective system was enormously successful but, like so many other new ideas, it was slow to penetrate the remote north-western counties. Indeed, it was not until 1739 that the first Trust was inaugurated to take responsibility for roads in the Whitehaven area, the spur clearly being the improvement of transport conditions between the coal mines and the harbour. The success of the venture set a precedent for further similar developments, but encouragement came from another quarter—the collapse of the 1745 Jacobite rebellion. Such were the difficulties in moving troops and supplies experienced by General Wade and the Duke of Cumberland that there was an immediate cry for urgent road improvements in the north. A direct result of this agitation was the construction of the Military Road linking Newcastle with Carlisle which, although designed for troops and military vehicles, encouraged industrial developments within the Carlisle region. In 1752 a Turnpike Trust was established for the road from Kendal through Kirkby Lonsdale and on to Keighley, followed in 1753 by a similar trust for the road from Heron Syke on the Westmorland boundary, through Kendal and Shap to Eamont Bridge. Further improvements followed quickly: the road from Kendal through Grayrigge and Orton to Appleby in 1760, and, a year later, the Kendal, Ambleside, Keswick,

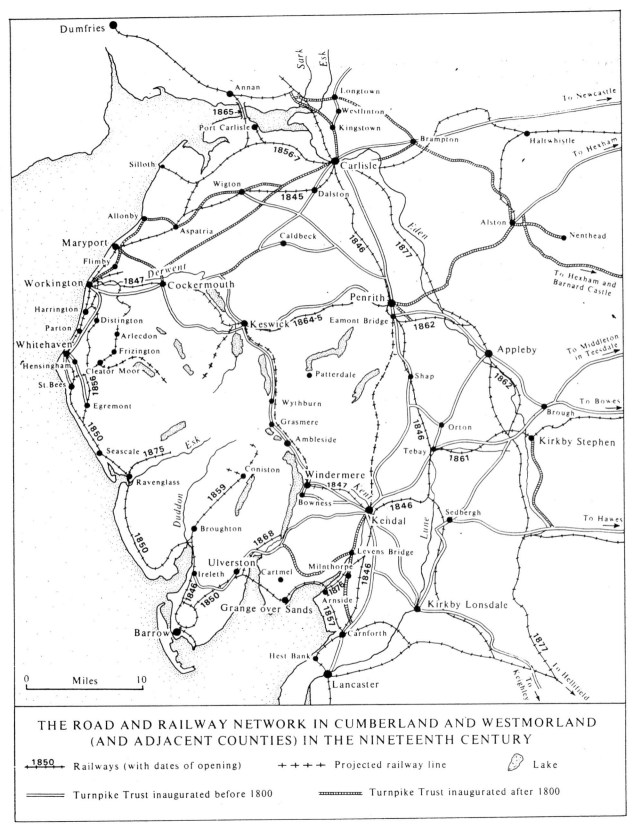

Dumfries
Annan
Longtown
To Newcastle
1865
Westlinton
Port Carlisle
Kingstown
Brampton
Haltwhistle
To Hexham
1856
Silloth
Carlisle
Wigton
Dalston
Alston
1845
Nenthead
Allonby
Aspatria
Caldbeck
Eden
To Hexham and
Barnard Castle
Maryport
1846
1877
Flimby
Derwent
Workington
1847
Cockermouth
Penrith
Harrington
Keswick 1864-5
Eamont Bridge
1862
To Middleton
in Teesdale
Parton
Distington
Appleby
Whitehaven
Arlecdon
Frizington
Patterdale
Shap
1862
To Bowes
Hensingham
Cleator Moor
St. Bees
1856
Wythburn
Brough
Egremont
Grasmere
Orton
Kirkby Stephen
1850
Ambleside
1846
Seascale 1875
Esk
Tebay
1861
To Hawes
Ravenglass
Coniston
1859
Windermere
Duddon
1847
Bowness
Kent
Broughton
1846
Kendal
Sedbergh
1868
Lune
1850
Ulverston
Ireleth
Cartmel
Milnthorpe
Levens Bridge
Grange over Sands
Arnside
1876
1846
Kirkby Lonsdale
Barrow
1846
1850
1857
Carnforth
1877
To Hellifield
Hest Bank
To Keighley
Lancaster

0   Miles   10

THE ROAD AND RAILWAY NETWORK IN CUMBERLAND AND WESTMORLAND
(AND ADJACENT COUNTIES) IN THE NINETEENTH CENTURY

1850 ──── Railways (with dates of opening)   + + + + Projected railway line   ◇ Lake

──── Turnpike Trust inaugurated before 1800   ▭▭▭▭ Turnpike Trust inaugurated after 1800

107 *Road and rail networks in the 19th century.*

Cockermouth road; also in 1761 the Kendal-Sedbergh Trust was inaugurated and this burst of turnpike mania concluded with the Act of 1763, which turnpiked the road from Kendal through Newby Bridge, Bouth, Penny Bridge to Ulverston and Ireleth, finally linking the isolated district of Lonsdale North of the Sands with the rest of England.

The effects of the improved turnpikes were both important and far-reaching. New forms of transport appeared to challenge the long-held supremacy of the pack-horse; in 1757 carriers' wagons appeared for the first time, and in 1763 the first stage coach, the *Flying Machine*, drawn by six horses, commenced its amazing service between Kendal and Carlisle over inhospitable Shap Fell at an almost incredible speed of between five and six miles an hour. Soon other

Kendal, Penrith, and Whitehaven
POST COACHES.

THE Proprietors of the GOOD INTENT and VOLUNTEER COACHES, return their sincere thanks to their Friends and the Public, for the liberal encouragement they have hitherto received, and respectfully inform them, that the

GOOD INTENT COACHES,
FROM KENDAL TO WHITEHAVEN,

Have commenced to run DAILY (Sundays excepted) by way of Ambleside, Keswick, Cockermouth, and Workington;—leaves Kendal at Five o'clock each morning, and Whitehaven at Eight, returning by the same route to Kendal.

THE VOLUNTEER

Leaves Penrith every Monday, Wednesday, and Friday morning at eight o'clock, and arrives in time at Keswick, to take the Kendal or Whitehaven Coaches, returning the same evening to Penrith.

PROPRIETORS:
JOHN JACKSON, Kendal.
WILLIAM WILCOCK, Ambleside.
WILLIAM ATKINSON, Penrith.
JOHN I'ANSON, Keswick.
WILLIAM WOOD, Cockermouth.

The Proprietors will not be accountable for any Package or Parcel above Five Pounds value, unless entered and paid for accordingly.
February 6, 1815.

108 *An early 19th-century coaching hand-bill.*

coaches, bearing such fanciful names as *The Royal Pilot, The True Briton,* and *The Good Intent*, entered into service to extend the network so that by the early decades of the 19th century even remote valleys such as Borrowdale had a coach service, and Cockermouth and Kendal were linked by a coach which struggled up the steep and stony Whinlatter Pass.

Revolutionary though this new mode of transport was, there were those who were less than enthusiastic. Indeed, one writer went so far as to add a cautionary tale of the doctors who 'warned people from travelling by the wild and whirling vehicle, as the rate at which it went would bring upon them all manner of strange disorders, chief among which was apoplexy'. But the learned doctors had little to fear, for on the whole the cost of travelling at the apparently dangerous speed of five miles per hour was prohibitive to all but the affluent and most dalesmen continued to travel on foot or on horseback as they had done for centuries. However, with the turnpiking of roads in the two counties and the consequent improved mobility, the ancient isolation of the area was breached; the first tourist hesitantly set foot in the Lakeland dales, Claude glass in one hand, Thomas West's *Guide* in the other, in search of 'the Picturesque'. By the mid-19th century the trickle of tourists had swollen to a flood and this increase in tourist traffic is reflected in the returns of the Ambleside Turnpike Trust for 1855, for in that year some 21,480 carriages crossed and re-crossed Troutbeck Bridge between Ambleside and Windermere and a further 15,240 paid the toll on the Grasmere to Keswick section of the road; yet 54 years earlier the passage of a single carriage along the road in front of Dove

Cottage was sufficiently noteworthy for Dorothy Wordsworth to record in her diary, 'Today a chaise passed'. The age of mass tourism, aided and abetted by the turnpike roads, had arrived.

The improved roads clearly encouraged visitors to venture into what was virtually *terra incognita*, yet until the 1770s there were few accurate maps showing roads. Most of the 18th-century maps of the two counties, though purporting to be 'new and accurate delineations', were simply slavish copies of Christopher Saxton's original surveys undertaken in the 16th century. Incorrect spelling and incredible errors were commonplace for they had been perpetuated for two centuries and, when roads were finally added to the already inaccurate maps, the result was at best misleading, at

109 *Part of Thomas Kitchin's map of Cumberland, 1777. Note the well-marked but non-existent road running from Great Langdale over the high fells to Wasdale Head and on to Whitehaven.*

worst, disastrous. Even Thomas Kitchin, 'Hydrographer to his Majesty', who engraved the maps for Nicolson and Burns's *History of Westmorland and Cumberland* in 1777, managed to 'invent' a large lake in Upper Eskdale, to mis-represent completely the Loweswater, Crummock and Buttermere group of lakes in such a way that they are unrecognisable, and to lead the unsuspecting traveller by a fictitious but cartographically well-marked and seemingly good road from Wrynose Pass to Wasdale Head over the highest and most difficult ground in England. Yet help for the bewildered and no doubt benighted traveller was at hand for in the 1770s the two counties were re-surveyed accurately on the scale of one inch to one mile, and cartographers such as Thomas Jefferys, Thomas Donald, and C. and J. Greenwood presented the visitor with truly reliable county maps, the worthy forerunners of the Ordnance Survey sheets.

Unfortunately, few rivers in Cumberland and Westmorland were navigable for any distance; moreover, the nature of the countryside dictated that the construction and maintenance of canals was uneconomic; consequently, the part played by inland navigation in the transport revolution is minimal. However, the story of the two canals, one in Cumberland, the other in Westmorland, should not be overlooked, for both made an impact on local trade and passenger transport. The more important of the two was the Lancaster Canal which had its origins in June 1791 when a group of Lancaster merchants approached the young engineer, John Rennie, to draw up plans for a canal which would connect Kendal and Lancaster with Westhoughton on the Lancashire coalfield. The main aim was simply to

110 *Part of Thomas Jefferys' map of Westmorland, 1770. Surveyed in 1768 by John Ainslie, this map marks an important turning point in the cartographic history of the two counties for it was the first truly accurate map. Drawn to a scale of one inch to the mile, it shows roads and mileage, churches and chapels, farms, mills and rough ground. Although altitude is not accurately depicted, relief is suggested by hachures.*

enhance the economic prospects of Lancaster and Kendal by facilitating the import of coal from the Wigan coalfield and the export of limestone and slates from the northern end of the canal to markets in south Lancashire. To this end an Act of Parliament was passed in 1792 and work on the canal commenced. The part Rennie himself played in the construction of the waterway is not clear, but it seems that by 1796 Thomas Fletcher was the engineer in charge of planning the Westmorland section. In 1797 the canal reached Tewitfield, 12 miles south of Kendal, but considerable capital was required to construct the locks necessary to carry the canal on to Kendal. The raising of this capital resulted in some delay so that it was not until the summer of 1819 that the northern section of the canal was opened. Although the southern section of the canal to Westhoughton was never completed, a light railway line connected the coalfield with the canal basin in Preston, so enabling the interchange of limestone and slate from the north with Lancashire's coal. As well as the transportation of bulky cargoes, the canal also served as a means of passenger transport, for on 1 May 1820 packet boats commenced a service between Kendal and Preston; the boats travelled at a sedate four miles an hour and passengers travelling from Preston boarded at six o'clock in the morning and arrived in Kendal at eight o'clock that night in time to catch the coach 'to the North'. The fare was six shillings in a fore cabin and four shillings in an aft cabin. By 1833 this leisurely but no doubt delightful service had been superseded by an express boat, the *Waterwitch*, which covered the 57 miles in seven hours with a change of horses every four miles. In spite of its apparent slowness, the service was initially successful; in its first six months it carried no fewer than 16,000 passengers between Preston and Kendal, and it remained in operation until the Lancaster and Carlisle railway was opened as far as Kendal in 1846.

The Carlisle Canal, like the Lancaster Canal, also traced its origin to the heady days of canal mania. In 1795 plans had been advanced for an ambitious project to link Newcastle by canal to the Solway Firth, a scheme which if completed would have materially improved the economic fortunes of Carlisle. Maryport was to have been the western terminus of this cross-country waterway, and, at a later date, a branch was to be constructed to Ullswater, so tapping the slate and mineral wealth of the Cumbrian mountains. Such a momentous project was doomed to failure largely by the fact that to cross the Tyne Gap alone would have required no fewer than 100 locks; however, the seeds of the idea had not fallen entirely on stony ground, for in 1818 the idea for a canal linking Carlisle with the sea was resurrected, plans were once again formulated and it was proudly announced that Carlisle would be transformed into 'the Emporium of north-west England'. The small coastal hamlet at Fisher's Cross, near Bowness, was chosen to replace Maryport as the Solway basin of the canal, and this was soon renamed Port Carlisle; work began on the 11½-mile navigation in 1819 and by March 1823 all was ready for the grand opening by civic dignitaries and a flotilla of small craft.

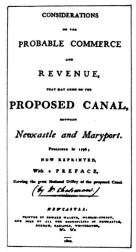

111 *Proposals for a Newcastle-Maryport canal.*

112 *Between 18,000 and 20,000 people witnessed the opening of the Carlisle Canal on 12 March 1823. Stretching 11¾ miles from Port Carlisle on the Solway to the city, the canal was at first successful but by the 1850s it had been superseded by railways and in 1854 it was transformed into a railway line.*

Carlisle celebrated its link to the sea with flags, salutes, patriotic songs and a gala dinner for shareholders, but the rejoicing was somewhat shortlived. Although the opening of the canal resulted in a reduction of the price of coal in the city and the opening of a small boat-building concern, it failed to meet the optimistic forecasts made at the opening. In an attempt to revive the waning fortunes of the canal, a passenger service was initiated in 1826 and this proved to be a partial success, perhaps because the vessel, the *Baillie Nichol Jarvie*, served not only as a packet boat but also as a floating bar. Eight years later she was replaced by the *Arrow*, a fly-boat some 66 ft. long and pulled by two horses, which covered the distance in one hour forty minutes at a cost of one shilling and sixpence. At Port Carlisle two steamers, the *Newcastle* and the *City of Carlisle*, picked up passengers and transferred them to Liverpool all within the same day, a journey which would have been impossible by road in the same time. A new note of optimism prevailed, and in 1840 new docks at Port Carlisle were opened, but in 1845 the opening of the Maryport and Carlisle Railway sounded the death knell and the final nail in the coffin was the completion of the Lancaster to Carlisle line shortly after, which created a through service to Liverpool, thus stripping the canal of the last of its passenger revenue. By the 1850s the canal was redundant, but in an amazing piece of metamorphism, it was drained, filled in and converted into a railway, thus helping Carlisle to become, if not a canal centre, then an important railway junction.

If the turnpikes of the 18th century helped to erode the isolation of the two counties, then the railways of the 19th furthered this process. The first public railway line in Cumberland—indeed, the first line to cross England from east to west—was the Newcastle and Carlisle Railway, completed in June 1838, and a few years later in 1845 the Maryport and Carlisle Railway was opened. Within the next two years the line between Maryport and Whitehaven (Bransty) was opened in stages, and by 1850 the Whitehaven and Furness Junction line had crossed the county boundary to Broughton in the Furness area of Lancashire to link up with the Furness Railway. Meanwhile, in Westmorland, Joseph Locke began the incredible feat of taking the main west coast line, the Lancaster and Carlisle Railway, over Shap Fell. George Stephenson in 1837 and John Hague in 1838 had both proposed that the main west coast line should be carried by embankments sweeping over Morecambe Bay and so along the West Cumberland coastal plain, but these plans were rejected in favour of the more direct though steeper route through the Lune Gorge. Parliament sanctioned the work in 1844, and by December 1846 the line was open to traffic, a feat to be marvelled at even in these days of heavy earth-moving equipment, but staggering when it is appreciated that the workforce consisted of almost 10,000 navvies and 1,000 horses working on some sections continuously on a 24-hour basis. The workforce consisted of Irish, Scottish, and English navvies in more or less equal proportions—a sure guarantee for friction— and there were many instances of trouble, the most serious disturbance being in Penrith in February 1846, when 2,000 men armed with shovels and picks ran riot and the Cumberland and Westmorland Yeomanry had to be called out to quell the trouble. However, despite these colourful incidents, the line was built with commendable speed, and the graceful Lowther and Eamont viaducts are splendid examples of Victorian civil engineering.

Until 1847 no railway penetrated into the Lake District proper but in that year two lines were built which, amid a clamour of opposition, reached out into the fells. In April 1847 the Cockermouth and Workington Railway was opened, and in the same month the Kendal and Windermere line reached Birthwaite, a small hamlet above Bowness-on-Windermere. The intention was to carry the lines on to Ambleside through Dunmail Raise and so to Keswick, but such plans did not materialise and the line terminated there, so resulting in the development of Windermere, a town which is as much a creation of the railway as Crewe or Swindon.

The impact of the railways was immediate for they acted as a catalyst to industrial and agricultural development. As early as 1838 merchants were

113 *A viaduct on the Kendal to Windermere railway line, 1847. Despite vociferous objections from William Wordsworth, who feared that the opening of the Kendal to Windermere railway would encourage 'the humbler classes to leave their homes', the line was opened in April 1847.*

buying eggs cheaply in Kendal market, taking them by cart to Carlisle, transferring them to Newcastle by rail from whence they were sent to London by sea. In 1847 a fortnightly cattle fair was started in Kendal, followed in 1849 by a similar one at Milnthorpe Station, the main aim being to provide fat cattle for the Manchester market. Carlisle's nodal position on the Solway plain endowed it not only with advantages as a railway junction but also as one of the most important livestock auction centres in the country. However, not all towns benefited from the railway age; until the opening in 1856 of the Carlisle and Silloth line most of the surplus agricultural produce of the Abbey Holme area was sent to Wigton market, but after the inauguration of the line, trade was diverted instead to Carlisle.

Surprisingly the railways had the effect of increasing traffic on the turnpike roads in some areas for many coach companies adjusted their schedules to connect with the new train services. Moreover, the railways heralded the age of mass tourism; at Windermere station excursion trains disgorged hordes of trippers from the industrial towns of Lancashire, and soon several farmers learned that it was more profitable to fleece tourists than sheep! The commercialisation of the Lake District, which had begun in a humble way in the late 18th century when 'the Lakers' came to gawp at the crags, was now stimulated by the coming of the railways.

114 *Windermere and the 'Rash Assault'. Despite vehement opposition from Wordsworth, the Kendal to Windermere railway was opened in 1847. However, his pragmatism overcame his aesthetic feelings when, in a letter to Charles Lloyd, he tentatively raised the question of investing a sum of up to £500 in railway companies. This lithograph, after J.B. Pyne, shows Windermere from Orrest Head—and a train leaving Windermere station (left).*

For many the railways brought prosperity, but there were others who entertained serious doubts about this new mode of travelling: 'no reasonable man would allow himself to be dragged through the air at the alarming rate of 20 miles per hour' trumpeted one antagonist and his views were shared by many. Others were more concerned with the social impact of railways; in a celebrated letter to *The Morning Post* in 1844, Wordsworth voiced his opposition to the 'rash assault' of the Kendal to Windermere line for he feared that the peace and tranquillity of the district would be shattered and the morals of the dales-folk threatened. He roundly condemned the directors of railway companies who were

> ... always ready to devise and encourage entertainments for tempting the humbler classes to leave their homes. Accordingly, for the profit of share-holder and that of the lower class of Innkeepers, we should have wrestling matches, horse and boat races without number and pot houses and beer shops would keep pace with these excitements and ... the injury which would thus be done to morals, both among this influx of strangers and the lower class of inhabitants is obvious.

Wordsworth, of course, was unsuccessful in his campaign, but in the 1870s the fight against the extension of the line from Windermere to Keswick was headed by John Ruskin and Robert Somervell. Ruskin assumed the same patronising attitude as Wordsworth when he wrote of 'the certainty of the deterioration of the moral character in the inhabitants of every district penetrated by a railway', and in a monumental piece of Victorian paternalism he wrote of the incoming tourists 'I do not wish them to see Helvellyn when they are drunk'.

The opposition to the 'Dunmail' line and to schemes to take railways into Ennerdale and Buttermere were successful, but not all influential literary voices were raised in protest against railways. Harriet Martineau, writing in 1855, expressed the view that 'any infusion of the intelligence and varied interest of the townspeople must ... be eminently beneficial' and she concluded that 'the best as well as the last and greatest change in the Lake District is that which is arising from the introduction of the railroad'.

Certainly the railways served to increase the tourist trade as well as to encourage an influx of *nouveaux riches* settlers who built for themselves mock-Gothic pantomime set-pieces on the shores of Windermere and elsewhere, but in addition this increased mobility and intercourse with new ideas and new techniques meant an alteration of a whole way of life and the decay of a venerable folk culture.

116 *Arcadia on the shores of Windermere. The paddle steamer* The Lady of the Lake *was launched on Windermere in 1845; Wordsworth was predictably outraged but the vessel proved popular with both residents and visitors and in her first short season she carried 5,000 passengers.*

12

Shipping and Shipbuilding

The proximity of Whitehaven to Ireland and its close involvement in the coal trade with that country clearly influenced the development of both shipping and shipbuilding in the vicinity of the town. Indeed, in the 17th century Sir John Lowther not only improved the harbour facilities but also attracted ship carpenters to the town, thereby assuring the future of an industry which remained important for two centuries. With the increased demand for coal from the Irish market so, too, there was a corresponding increase in Whitehaven's shipping; in 1676 the town had a fleet of 32 ships; six years later the number had increased to 40, and in 1685 the total had reached 46 ships. In that year Whitehaven achieved the status of a customs port and assumed responsibility for the Cumberland coast from Ravenglass to Ellenfoot (Maryport). Although coal remained the chief item of trade, in the last quarter of the 17th century Whitehaven extended its commercial links with America and the resulting importation of Virginian tobacco developed into a profitable venture. By the beginning of the 18th century the town was one of a dozen ports allowed to import tobacco, and so trade flourished; in 1712 some 1,639,193lbs. of tobacco were shipped into Whitehaven, but by 1740 this had increased to 4,419,218lbs. The ships used in this trade were not large—Richard Kelsick's *Resolution* with a keel length of 60ft. was the largest vessel—and the round trip to Virginia and back took the best part of a year; nevertheless, fortunes were made in the Americas trade and families such as the Gales, Blacklocks, Lutwidges, and the Martins owed much of their new-found prosperity to Virginia tobacco. By the 1720s and 1730s, however, West Cumberland merchants began to feel the cold wind of competition from Glasgow as more and more of the lucrative tobacco trade found its way to the Clyde rather than to Cumberland. The final blow fell with the American War of Independence, so that by the beginning of the 19th century the import of tobacco was no longer signifi-cant, as Parson and White's *Directory* for 1829 makes clear: 'formerly about 20,000 hogsheads of tobacco were annually imported here from Virginia but now scarce a fourth part of that number, Glasgow having stolen that branch'.

However, despite the loss of a once important commodity, the port continued to flourish. During the first quarter of the 18th century the tonnage of Whitehaven shipping increased from approximately 4,000 tons to over 9,000 tons, and this figure was further increased by as much again during the next 25 years. Although it seems that the tonnage for such places as Ravenglass, Workington, and Maryport are included in these figures, since these harbours were officially attached to Whitehaven, nevertheless this remarkable increase is adequate testimony to the growing importance of shipping in West Cumberland. Throughout the whole of the 18th century the shipping returns indicate Whitehaven's emergence as a serious rival to Bristol and Liverpool; indeed, in 1744 the town's shipping figures actually exceeded those of Liverpool—17,485 tons as opposed to Liverpool's 15,932. By 1790 Whitehaven registered some 448 vessels which employed 3,451 seamen, and this compared favourably with the much larger city of Liverpool which registered 479 vessels in the same year.

117 The brig Love of Whitehaven, *1745. This bowl, probably made in Liverpool, commemorated the launching of the* Love *at Whitehaven. In 1746 she sailed to Virginia and was almost certainly involved in the tobacco trade.*

In 1725 Daniel Defoe described Whitehaven as

grown up from a small place to be very considerable by the coal trade, which is increased so considerably of late, that it is now the most eminent port in England for shipping of coals except Newcastle and Sunderland, and even beyond the last, for they wholly supply the city of Dublin, and all the towns of Ireland on that coast.

Even allowing for Defoe's customary superlatives, it would appear that the development of Whitehaven's shipping was extraordinary; moreover, within the 18th century the population of the town grew fourfold, from 2,222 in 1693 to 9,063 in 1762, and even as late as 1816 Whitehaven was recognised as one of the largest towns in the north of England. However, by the early 19th century geographical factors asserted themselves and the fortunes of the town were reversed. Whereas Liverpool had a thriving, developing hinterland made up of the Lancashire cotton towns, Whitehaven possessed only the fells which served to cut off West Cumberland from the towns on the eastern side of the country. In the final analysis, the absence of an economically important hinterland proved critical, and Whitehaven declined in the face of increasing competition from the Mersey.

Yet this decline was not a rapid one, since the coal trade had stimulated the shipbuilding industry and by the end of the 18th century there were shipyards in all the Cumbrian ports. Indeed, it has been calculated that about half the total number of Cumberland ships in 1786 had been launched from local slipways. Many of these wooden ships were small—the *Ferret*, built at Whitehaven in 1783, was a mere nine tons—but others such as the *Carlisle*, launched in the same year, were over 220 tons, and the average tonnage of a Cumberland ship at this time was 118 tons. In the later part of the 18th century and the early decades of the 19th, the ship-yards of West Cumberland continued to launch ships which not only entered into the coastal trade but also sailed to America, the Mediterranean and the Baltic, and most of these vessels were owned by groups of investors—merchants, mariners, tanners, blacksmiths, shopkeepers, even yeoman farmers and widows.

Without question, the best-known of Whitehaven's shipbuilders was Daniel Brocklebank. Born in 1742 at Torpenhow where his father was curate-in-charge of the parish church, in 1770 he emigrated to Sheepscutt, Maine, where he established a small shipbuilding yard. Caught in the turmoil of the American War of Independence, he returned home to his native Cumberland and settled in Whitehaven where he established the famous Brocklebank shipping line. Between 1782, when he founded his shipbuild-ing yard, and his death in 1801, he built 27 ships. Daniel's two sons, Thomas and John, carried on the business, but in 1819 a commercial link with Liverpool was forged which later proved powerful enough to attract the company to the Mersey. Brocklebanks continued to build ships at Whitehaven until 1865, but in that year the lease of the yard expired and the ties were finally broken. At Workington, John Wood seems to have

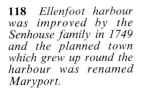

118 *Ellenfoot harbour was improved by the Senhouse family in 1749 and the planned town which grew up round the harbour was renamed Maryport.*

established a shipyard prior to 1756, so establishing an association which lasted some 60 years, and nine years later his brother William set up a yard at Maryport which dominated shipbuilding there for over a century. By 1829 Harrington, Maryport, and Workington had two shipyards each, and Whitehaven, significantly, had six.

Not surprisingly, other industries closely allied to shipbuilding flourished in the late 18th and early 19th centuries. Naturally, shipbuilding required an abundant supply of timber, but the woodland resources of Cumberland had long been depleted, so timber had to be imported from such ports as Danzig, Riga, Memel, and Elsinore. In addition to wood for the shipbuilding industry, timber was needed for wooden wagon rails and 'linings' in the collieries, as well as for the 'clog soles' for the wicker corves used to transport the coal to the surface. When the French Wars prevented the import of timber from the Baltic, other sources had to be hastily found, and John Christian Curwen was first obliged to buy supplies from the Loch Moidart area in Scotland and later from Barmouth and Dolgellau in Wales. A brisk trade developed with the Mawddach estuary and ships taking timber to West Cumberland brought back cargoes of coal and haematite. Shipbuilding also called for ropes and sails, and by the end of the 18th century both Workington and Whitehaven had well-established rope-walks and sail-lofts, the hemp being imported from St Petersburg. When steam-ships replaced sailing ships, the sailmaking industry suffered a grievous blow, but it lingered on in Whitehaven until the 1930s.

Although Westmorland possessed but a short length of coastline, the county did have one port—Milnthorpe. Insignificant by comparison with Whitehaven, nevertheless Milnthorpe could trace its origins as a port at least until the end of the 16th century. According to the Duchy of Lancaster Index of Patents, in 1589 one 'Barnabye Bennyson hath the colleccon of all such groundage wharfage and other dutyes as shall growe due to her

119 *Low tide, Whitehaven harbour, c.1856. The Harrington-registered* Bee *(left) is berthed next to the* Favourite *of Whitehaven (right). Although coal remained the most important industry in 19th-century Whitehaven, shipbuilding and ancillary trades continued to flourish.*

Ma(jes)tie for casting Anker uppon her Ma(jes)ties soyle of the common called Haverbrack or Milnethorpe haven and landinge of wares there'. However, until the 18th century, little is known of the commercial activity of this small port at the mouth of the River Bela. Being the nearest port to Kendal, Milnthorpe was of some importance to that town; much of the 'cole' used in Kendal's flourishing 18th-century industries was imported through Milnthorpe and in 1729 the Corporation of Kendal petitioned the Lords of the Treasury for the remission of duties on coal imported through the port, but their lordships remained obdurate and the petition was rejected.

Coal was not the only item of trade; salt, both for agricultural purposes and to supply the needs of Kendal manufacturers, was imported from Liverpool and Northwich. Pig iron from Scotland was also brought into Milnthorpe *en route* for the small forge at Sedgwick, and grain to supply the many water mills in this area further increased the trade of the port. Towards the end of the 18th century the newly-established gunpowder industry of the Kent valley brought Milnthorpe to the height of its prosperity as a port. Saltpetre from India and sulphur from Sicily and Italy were brought from Liverpool to the mouth of the River Bela in small coasting vessels which were unloaded onto wooden carts for the final leg of the journey to the gunpowder mills. Similarly, Milnthorpe was the main port of export for the black powder and a service developed between the port and Liverpool, carrying not only gunpowder for the powder magazines at the mouth of the Mersey, but also some passengers. The early years of the 19th century were prosperous, but the fat years were followed by lean ones which heralded the decline and eventual extinction of Milnthorpe as a port. In 1819 the Kendal-Lancaster canal was opened, with dire consequences for the small Westmorland port; trade dwindled to a mere fraction of its former importance and 38 years later the final blow fell when the Furness Railway line between Ulverston and Carnforth crossed the Kent estuary on a viaduct which in effect prevented navigation beyond Arnside.

XII *Farming at Burnthwaite, Wasdale Head. Here the good quality 'inland' pasture on the valley floor contrasts with the thin, stony soils of the steep fellsides.*

XIII *Haverigg, South Cumberland. This modern development at Haverigg, near Millom, provides a new face for a 19th-century iron mining area.*

13

The Iron Industry in Cumberland

Two minerals helped to shape the industrial destiny of West Cumberland; one was coal, and the other was the rich red haematite iron ore won from the silver-grey Carboniferous Limestone which lies between the coal-bearing rocks and the fringes of the Lake District uplands. In the 19th century this iron-mining area, occupying a narrow strip from Haile in the south to Lamplugh in the north, was a thriving, noisy industrial region where life was governed by the rhythmic heartbeat of the pumping engine and the insistent, inharmonious sound of the mine hooter, and where the small surface streams were discoloured by haematite pollution. Today the industrial phase is long past, but, like coal mining, the exploitation of iron ore has left its pock-marks on the landscape, a legacy of flooded, abandoned pits, overgrown spoil tips, disused mineral lines choked with willow-herb, and rows of terraced mining cottages which, in spite of losing their *raison d'être*, possess some of the finest views of the Lakeland fells to be found anywhere in Cumbria.

Yet it would be wrong to think of iron-mining as a purely 19th-century activity; indeed, the history of haematite mining in Cumberland is as long as that of coal-mining, going back at least to the 12th century. Sometime in that century the monks of St Bees were granted an iron mine at Acknirby, near Egremont, and about 1179 the brethren at Holm Cultram received a gift from William, 3rd Earl of Albemarle, of a forge at Whinfell, near Lorton, and an iron mine at Egremont. From the available evidence, then, it appears that Egremont was the centre of the early medieval iron industry and in the 14th century there are references to several iron forges located near to the market place. It is unlikely, however, that the mining of haematite occurred at any great depth below the surface and it seems that most of the ore was won from shallow bell-pits.

Mining techniques changed little, even by the 17th century; the Rev. Thomas Robinson, rector of Ouseby, describes a visit to an iron mine at Langhorn, near Egremont, at the end of that century, and comments that the haematite was close to the surface and was worked in an opencast manner like a stone quarry. He goes on to record the nature of the ore:

> In a place called Langhorn within that Manor [Egremont] is a Belly or Pipe of Iron
> Ore eight yards deep, in breadth 80 yards and in length a hundred; out of which

several thousand Tun were yearly got for many years ... the ore was very rich consisting of Button ore and a pinguid shining ore.

Although the documentary evidence is slight, there can be no doubt that other similar mines were being worked in the neighbourhood at the same period; for example, in 1670 it seems that a certain William Coates let 'all his iron mine, iron weare, iron oare, and iron stone, lying, and being within his freehold estate at Woodend', near Cleator, to Thomas Patrickson of Ennerdale, and there is reason to believe that the same mine was being worked 12 years later. Similarly, towards the end of the 17th century the royalties received by the Duke of Somerset, the owner of the Nicholson iron ore pits near Egremont, increased considerably, a sure indication of further exploration and exploitation, and in 1694 a letter from William Gilpin of Scaleby to Sir John Lowther refers to 'free and plentiful ore at Langaran, near Whitehaven, and that at Frizington and the intended forge at Cleator, for smelting them with pit coal'. This last phrase is significant since it suggests that even as early as the 17th century attempts were being made to capitalise on the juxtaposition of coal and iron by smelting with coal; the experiments were rather premature, however, for the technical difficulties were not completely overcome until the early decades of the next century.

Until the early 18th century, most of the iron mined in Cumberland was smelted in crude 'bloomeries' and 'bloomsmithies' where charcoal was

120 *Duddon Bridge Iron Furnace, Cumberland, 1736-1867. Situated on the Cumberland side of the river Duddon, the ruins of this once important chacoal-fired blast furnace are among the most impressive industrial monuments in Britain. Using haematite iron ore from the mines of Low Furness and local charcoal the furnace worked for between 20 and 30 weeks; every 12 hours about 10 tonnes of molten iron was tapped out of the hearth onto the sand-filled casting floor.*

KEY:
1 *Pine and iron water-wheel, 27 ft. in diameter*
2 *Cast-iron blowing cylinders, installed in 1785*
3 *Blowing Arch*
4 *Casting Arch-slag and molten iron tapped off*
5 *Furnace temperature 1,500 degrees centigrade*
6 *Cast-iron 'pigs'*
7 *Slag*
8 *Furnace mouth—fed by a 'charge' of charcoal, haematite iron ore and a small amount of limestone.*

the main smelting agent. In 1736, on the banks of the River Duddon near Duddon Bridge, a significant development occurred when the Duddon Iron Furnace began production. Using haematite ore from the mines of Low Furness which was transported along the Duddon estuary by shallow-draughted boats, charcoal from local woods, and with bellows powered by water from the river, the furnace was very favourably sited. The pig iron cast here was sent to Chepstow and Bristol where it was used in the manufacture of anchors, chains and other iron work for ships. Until it was closed in 1867, the furnace underwent little alteration to its basic design— the original ox-hide bellows were replaced by blowing cylinders in 1785, but these continued to be operated by water power. Although the building is now roofless and silent, surrounded in spring by a carpet of bluebells, it is undoubtedly one of the most impressive charcoal-fired blast furnaces in Britain and a fitting memorial to the charcoal iron industry in Cumberland.

By the middle of the 18th century, coke-fired furnaces were increasing in number. In 1750 blast furnaces were built at Little Clifton, on the banks of the river Marron, which supplied the water power necessary for the bellows; coal was supplied from the nearby mines at Clifton and Greysouthen, and haematite was transported on the backs of pack-horses from the mines at Frizington. Shortly after, in 1752, a blast furnace was in operation at Mote Hill, Maryport, and in 1762 the most successful of all the 18th-century Cumberland furnaces was established at Seaton on the river Derwent. Founded by one of the most outstanding ironmasters of West Cumberland, James Spedding of Whitehaven, the plant consisted of two blast furnaces, slitting and rolling mills, and a foundry in which were cast ships' guns, cannon, fire grates, various types of hollowware, and several steam engines. The venture prospered, and by 1794 it employed several hundred men and was one of the largest iron manufactories in the north of England. By the end of the century blast furnaces had been blown at Lowca, north of Whitehaven, and at Frizington on the ore-field, but little is known of their history. With the exception of the Seaton plant, these early experiments with blast furnaces were not entirely successful, mainly because of the unsuitability of the local coal for metallurgical purposes

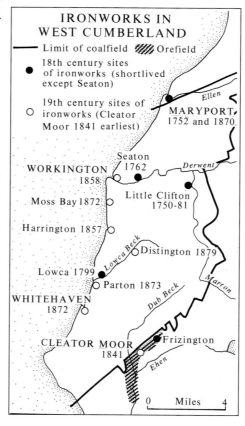

121 *Ironworks in West Cumberland.*

and the unreliability of water power to drive the bellows. Consequently, most of the works were abandoned after a short period.

Although this first blast furnace phase was abortive, the increased mining of haematite demonstrated the richness of that ore and soon Cumberland iron had gained a reputation far beyond the boundaries of the county. At the end of the century, mines such as that at Crowgarth, near Egremont, were producing rich ore from a depth of only 12 fathoms, yet before 1784 the deposit had scarcely been worked, and this pattern was repeated in other mines. In the 12 months between 1790 and 1791 more than 20,000 tons of ore were exported through such ports as Whitehaven and Parton, some of it to South Wales, Wrexham, and Shropshire, but considerable quantities going north of the border to the famous Carron Iron Works near the Clyde, then one of the foremost blast furnace plants in Europe. Significant though this expansion undoubtedly was, the great breakthrough point came as the result of a technological development in the mid-19th century; in 1856 Henry Bessemer first publicised his famous process for making steel, an innovation which revolutionised the industry. However, this 'convertor' demanded that the iron used should be free of phosphorus and fortune dictated that Cumberland had the only extensive deposits of non-phosphoric ores in the kingdom; consequently, between 1856 and 1878 when the Gilchrist-Thomas process made possible the use of phosphoric ores, Cumberland haematite was much in demand and the area held a monopoly control of the market. With ill-concealed delight, Lord Leconfield's estate agent was able to write in 1870 that '... the red haematite from this district must always maintain its superiority ... the steel makers now find it absolutely essential for their particular purpose'. Although he was not altogether correct in his belief, for the smelting of phosphoric ore after 1878 and the import of cheap Spanish ore in the 1880s helped to erode the supremacy of Cumberland haematite, nevertheless the fact remains that the '60s, '70s and '80s were the boom years, and the impact on the economy and the landscape of the area was considerable.

In spite of the relative failure of most of the 18th-century blast furnaces, the locally-based iron and steel industry assumed a new lease of life after 1842 and the output from the mines increased to keep pace with these developments. In 1841 the Whitehaven Iron and Steel Company was established and shortly after they opened a furnace at Cleator Moor, a short distance from the village of Cleator; few could have foreseen the industrial developments which followed in the wake of the blowing-in of this plant. Within a decade a new industrial village had developed around the works, and men from Ireland, Scotland, the Isle of Man, Cornwall, Northumberland, Lancashire, and Yorkshire flocked to the area to mine the ore and to tend the furnaces. Just as the development of the Carlisle-Maryport railway had stimulated the mining of coal in the first half of the century, so, too, the construction of the line from Whitehaven to Cleator and Egremont in 1856 and its subsequent extension to Rowrah and Lamplugh gave additional impetus to the iron industry. By the 1870s the haematite mines were of national importance and the annual output of iron

122 *A 'Duck lamp'*
used in iron mines.

ore averaged over one million tons and a maximum of 1,725,478 tons was reached in 1882, a year in which West Cumberland contributed 12 per cent of the national production of pig iron. One of the most important workings opened during this period was the Montreal mine, east of Cleator Moor; between 1870 and 1880 this one mine alone produced over two million tons of haematite but, because of a geological accident, the same shaft also produced coal, an occurrence almost unique in Great Britain. Not far away, the rich Parkside mine exploited one of the largest haematite deposits in the area, producing over 150,000 tons in 1874, and after 1877 the iron veins in the Silurian rocks of the Murton and Kelton Fells further supplemented the output from the mines on the Carboniferous Limestones.

Clearly, such sudden and dramatic industrial expansion was accompanied by an equally startling increase in the population; between 1840 and 1880 industrial villages such as Frizington, Arlecdon, Cleator, and Cleator Moor grew in response to the development of the iron industry and within these 40 years the population of the area rose from 835 to 17,651, and the number of miners increased from 60 to over six thousand. The census returns for 1801, 1851, and 1901 tell the same story:

	1801	1851	1901
{ Arlecdon	354	643	1,632 }
{ Frizington			3,709 }
Cleator Moor	362	1,779	8,120
{ Egremont	1,515	2,049	3,599 }
{ Bigrigg			2,162 }
Workington	5,716	6,280	26,143

123 *Iron miner's clogs. The alder soles afforded insulation from the damp ground.*

Yet these figures are mere bald statistics; they convey nothing of the social problems, the overcrowding, or the deprivation which attended the birth and growth of these industrial communities. They give no impression of the hard-working—and hard-drinking—men who often created in these West Cumberland villages an atmosphere and a social environment more appropriate to the gold-mining settlements of North America than to the north of England. Neither can they illuminate the tensions which developed between the immigrant groups, particularly the Irish and Scots, and the 'locals', who regarded with suspicion any 'off-comers' from outside West Cumberland. Nor can these printed figures tell of the casualties and the anguish which accompanied the various mining tragedies for, like the coal mines on the coast, the iron-mining field had its share of injuries and fatalities, part of the sad but inevitable price paid for 19th-century prosperity.

In the 1870s and '80s two other iron mining centres began production; one proved to be of limited importance, but the other developed into one of the most productive haematite areas in Britain. In 1872 several veins of iron ore were discovered near Boot, in Eskdale, and in spite of the comparative remoteness it was felt that they should be exploited; between 1872 and 1883 some 59,000 tons of ore were removed, principally from the vein known as 'Nab Gill', but conditions proved to be more difficult than at first anticipated. The ore occurs in the Eskdale granites, but deposits are irregular and variable in quality, making profitable working difficult. After 1883 mining ceased and the visitor to this most beautiful Lakeland valley has to look carefully to discover the characteristic evidence of mining activity. One distinctive feature yet remains; the Ravenglass and Eskdale Railway, affectionately known to generations of children as 'l'ile Ratty', and much esteemed by their fathers, was originally built as a mineral line to transport the iron ore to the main West Cumberland line at Ravenglass. First opened in 1875, the line was relaid on a 15in. gauge in 1915 and today it carries thousands of tourists and local people, providing an important element in the public transport network as well as a tourist attraction.

If the Eskdale ores did not live up to expectations, the ores at Hodbarrow, at the southern tip of Cumberland, proved to be considerably more productive than anyone could have anticipated. Although haematite may have been mined in this area at the end of the 17th century, the earliest 19th-century exploration seems to have commenced about 1845 when the Earl of Lonsdale began a limited operation. Meeting with little success, he abandoned the venture but allowed the newly-formed Hodbarrow Mining Company to continue exploration. In 1856 the first major deposit of haematite was discovered and exploitation began; 10 years later some 265 men were employed underground, but the major discovery of the richest single haematite body in England was still some years away. By 1868 it was apparent that considerable quantities of ore extended for an unknown distance under the estuary of the Duddon and as exploitation extended southwards towards high water mark the risk of subsidence and subsequent flooding by the sea increased. In an attempt to avert such an occurrence the Hodbarrow Mining Company erected a wooden barrier in 1885; then, in 1888, work commenced on a sea wall, the so-called Inner Barrier, designed to prevent inundation of the workings at high tide. With the completion of this sea wall, underground workings were rapidly extended seaward, for it allowed the extraction of between four and five million tons of ore; indeed, between March 1892 and March 1893 nearly 540,000 tons of haematite were raised, the largest annual output since the opening of the mine.

The Inner Barrier certainly extended the life of the mine, but within a few years surface subsidence began to affect the massive structure; in May 1898 the situation became serious when a 'run' of wet sand rushed into the workings and was followed by subsidence of alarming proportions. Emergency repairs were undertaken but it soon became apparent that, if the mine was to be saved, the construction of a second sea wall, the Outer Barrier, was essential. Work began in 1900 and continued until 1905 when finally this most impressive piece of civil engineering was completed. Something in excess of a mile in length, the barrier extended from Haverigg to Hodbarrow Point and was composed of rubble limestone and clay protected by enormous concrete blocks weighing 25 tons each, and iron slag. Although

the total cost of the Outer Barrier was almost £600,000, it not only protected the existing workings but also extended mining operations seaward once more. Between 1905 and 1908 haematite production exceeded 500,000 tons a year, but thereafter a steady and inexorable decline set in; the realisation that even Hodbarrow had a limited potential precipitated a mood of uncertainty which ultimately gave way to pessimism. Some 13 million tons of iron ore had been won from the Hodbarrow mine by 1900, but by 1958 the annual output had shrivelled to a mere 40,000 tons, and 10 years later mining finally ceased. The land enclosed by the Outer Barrier had already assumed that characteristic appearance of dereliction, and the area became a sad, contorted, melancholy landscape dotted with subsidence craters, overgrown with hawthorn and bramble and crossed by the remains of the Inner Barrier like a miniature Great Wall of China as it roller-coastered over the broken and subsided ground. When the pumps finally ceased working, the water rose and a huge lake was created so that today it is a nature reserve and a sanctuary for a wide variety of wildfowl and seabirds.

124 *Hodbarrow, Cumberland. The building of the Inner Barrier, designed to prevent inundation of the iron workings at high tide. In the background an earlier wooden barrier may be seen. This photograph was taken about 1890.*

14

The Nineteenth-Century Urban Scene

It has been said, with considerable justification, that the decade between 1850 and 1860 marked a watershed in the history of man's contribution to the developing landscape of the Lake counties. Certainly in the early part of the century the economy was essentially rural and the steady pace of life was governed by the seasons, by seed-time and harvest, by lambing and clipping, as it had been for centuries. In the second half of the century the process of change clearly accelerated; the percentage of urban dwellers increased and entirely new towns came into being. By 1857 it was possible to travel by rail from Carlisle along the West Cumberland coast, through Furness and Cartmel to Carnforth and then return to Carlisle via the railway over Shap Fell, and by the beginning of the 20th century the early motor cars made perilous ascents of Lakeland passes. In short, the isolation of the area had finally been broken down, and the process begun by the turnpike roads of the 18th century and hastened by the railways of the 19th was ultimately completed by the internal combustion engine. Yet the 19th century was a period when the old and the new were juxtaposed in a remarkable way; in the 1840s, when Victorian tourists were being smoothly conveyed along the recently-opened Kendal to Windermere railway line at an incredible average speed of 24 miles per hour, gangs of pack-horses were still plodding their way from Kendal to Whitehaven.

Although the population of the two counties increased considerably during the second half of the 18th century, it grew even more rapidly in the early decades of the 19th. Between 1800 and 1831 the population of Cumberland rose by 45.5 per cent from 116,639 to 169,681, and that of Westmorland by 32.3 per cent from 41,605 to 55,041. Moreover, within these 30 years the population became more urban; in 1801 the four towns of Carlisle, Whitehaven, Penrith and Keswick contained some 20 per cent of Cumberland's population, but by 1831 this had increased to 23.3 per cent. Similarly, in Westmorland in 1801 Kendal, Appleby, Kirkby Lonsdale and Kirkby Stephen accounted for 29 per cent of the population, but this figure increased to 31 per cent by 1831. However, it should be said that by 20th-century standards none of these towns was large; in 1831 Carlisle, with 20,000, was the most populous, followed by Whitehaven with 17,000, but Appleby had a mere 2,723, and Keswick fewer than 2,200 citizens.

Indeed, the towns of the early 19th century retained a rural character and even in Carlisle the sound of sheep and cattle in the streets was a familiar one.

In the second half of the 19th century the picture changed somewhat and in many cases a sharp increase in the number of urban dwellers gave rise to overcrowding and related health hazards. By 1850, Carlisle had long since outgrown the confines of the ancient city walls and linear suburbs extended finger-like along Botchergate, Rickergate and Caldewgate, the three main routes into the town; but within the city centre overcrowding became acute, and hundreds of people lived in dark, insanitary courts, the worst of which were described by one observer as 'the receptacles of every kind of filth ... containing almost invariably pigsties, open privies, dunghills [and] stagnant pools'. The growth of such industries as textiles, brewing, biscuit-making and other manufacturing activities, together with the rise of the city as a railway junction of national importance, further stimulated urban growth, and the industrial suburb of Denton Holme developed along the flat valley floor of the River Caldew. Dr. Alan Harris has calculated that in 1851 some 780 people lived in the district of Denton Holme, but 10 years later 2,800 people were crowded into the same area, most of them living in courts and 'back to back' houses.

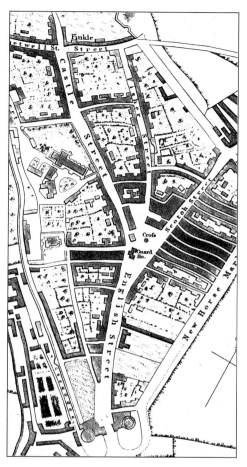

125 *Central Carlisle, 1815. The market cross may be identified in the centre of the map. During the recent development of The Lanes shopping centre, to the right of the market cross, the remains of two large wooden-built Roman buildings were discovered.*

But Carlisle was not the only Cumberland town to suffer the blight of 19th-century urban squalor; Whitehaven, too, experienced over-crowding and poverty to such a degree that the promising image of a well-planned 'new town' was irrevocably tarnished. In 1858 one observer was moved to write:

> There is only one street in England that we have seen to beat Quay Street, Whitehaven, for squalor and filth, and that was Lace Street, Liverpool, before the sanitary act came into operation . ..
>
> Houses, shops, jerry shops, courts, public houses, everything you come on speaks plainly of overcrowding. Sallow-looking women covered with rags, thrust their heads and half their bodies through the windows to look after you, and as they do this they appear to gasp for fresh air.

Parts of early 19th-century Kendal likewise earned an unsavoury reputation; in Moffat's Court, off Stricklandgate, 120 people lived in 35 cottages, with only two privies to serve them. In another yard were 18 cottages with 75 residents, a bakehouse, seven pigsties, and several dung-heaps and cesspools. Not surprisingly, such conditions provided virulent breeding grounds for cholera during the outbreak of 1832. Even as late as 1849 when Kendal had 2,900 inhabited houses, only 90 had taps. This depressing picture was much the same at Penrith, but by the late 1840s some changes were being made; a second epidemic of cholera in 1848-49 taught the middle classes that the disease was no respecter of class and that the flies which visited the crowded courts and pigsties impartially visited their houses also. Reforms were demanded, and under the Public Health Act provisions were made for better drainage, water supplies and sewage disposal so that by the turn of the century the general urban environment had undergone some improvement.

However, there were exceptions and the development of Millom, in South Cumberland, gave rise to certain planning problems; originally envisaged as 'a sort of model town', plans for the new community were ambitious; in 1867 the local ironworks was inaugurated when two blast furnaces were blown in, but later additions increased the number of furnaces to six. Although rows of terraced houses were soon built, the influx of immigrants far outstripped the available accommodation and inevitably gross overcrowding followed; houses were often occupied by two or more families, and, in the graphic words of one newspaper, '... in scores of houses the beds were never cold'. In 1871, the population of Millom and the older nucleus of Holborn Hill reached 3,000 and smallpox and typhus followed in the wake of the overcrowded and insanitary housing conditions. Three years later one of the most crowded and ill-drained sections of the town was described by the local Medical Officer as:

> ... a reproach and antithesis to even a remotely sanitary state ... the drainage in many places consisting of sweltering, stagnant puddle-holes in which may be seen floating the carcases of drowned cats and puppies ... the backyard receptacles for house refuse, night soil and ash, unroofed and some filled to overflowing; pigs and goats roaming ... horses going at large ...

Under such conditions, then, the brave hopes for a 'model town' turned sour. However, assisted by the Cumberland Iron Mining and Smelting Company, which controlled the iron works, and the Hodbarrow Mining Company, social and environmental improvements occurred in the late 1870s, churches, chapels, and schools were built, and a market hall, shops, and a hotel endowed the town with a new status and sense of community.

Of course, not all towns suffered industrial urbanism to this degree, but many experienced the development of 'artisan housing'. By the early decades of the century, most of Kendal's famous yards had been converted into industrial sites concerned with the woollen industry, complete with small cottages for the workers, but after the arrival of the railway in 1847 the station formed the centre of a new area of housing. A similar pattern

RICHER WILL BE THE VALE OF EDEN

SUCCESS TO THE EDEN VALLEY RAILWAY

emerged at Appleby; in 1862 the Eden Valley Railway was opened, to be followed in 1876 by the completion of the Carlisle and Settle line. Appleby then found itself possessed of two railway stations, both on the eastern side of the town, and around them a new housing complex soon developed.

At Windermere, on the other hand, a different type of housing was brought into being by the railway, for here members of the upper middle-class built their villas and created Arcadia overlooking the lake. By the end of the century the former hamlet had assumed the proportions of a town and the introduction of the Windermere Express made it possible for tired businessmen to travel in little over two hours to their rural retreats after a hard day in the Manchester Cotton Exchange. But in addition to being an early example of a commuter settlement, Windermere also developed as a tourist centre, for the railway made it possible for many middle-class visitors to enjoy Lakeland holidays and soon hotels, boarding houses and 'lodging houses' were catering for all tastes. Bowness, the older settlement on the lake shore, also participated in this newly-found prosperity, and in 1883 local directories indicated that there were 45 boarding house keepers in Windermere and 43 in Bowness. Keswick, too, followed an identical

126 *Appleby, Westmorland, 1858. To mark the cutting of the first sod of the Eden Valley Railway, this triumphal arch was erected in Westmorland's county town. The line was finally opened in 1862.*

pattern; although the Cockermouth, Keswick and Penrith Railway was primarily intended to facilitate the transportation of coking coal to the furnaces of West Cumberland, when the line was opened in 1864, a new influx of tourists created a demand for additional accommodation. To meet this, the *Keswick Hotel* was opened in 1869, a splendid Victorian pile equal in grandeur to those other railway-inspired hotels, the *Windermere Hotel* and the *Grange Hotel* in North Lancashire. In addition, of course, scores of smaller hotels and boarding houses capitalised on the thousands of tourists who were annually decanted onto the platforms of the Keswick railway station; in 1878 some 150,000 third-class passengers arrived in the town by train, but four years later this figure had increased to 240,000.

However, the arrival of the railway did not always bring with it hoards of eager tourists, and the history of Seascale on the Cumberland coast proved to be a timely lesson to planners and speculators. The Whitehaven and Furness Junction Railway was opened from Whitehaven to Ravenglass in 1849 and a temporary station was constructed at Seascale, a small but remote sea-bathing resort. In July 1870 the directors of the Furness Railway Company, which had acquired the Whitehaven line in 1866, accepted proposals for the transformation of the hamlet into a genteel seaside town complete with boulevards, promenades, and crescents to equal anything offered by Bournemouth or Eastbourne. Clearly heartened by their attempts to turn Grange-over-Sands and the adjacent coasts of Morecambe Bay into a Lancashire Riviera, the directors engaged Edward Kemp, who had just completed the laying-out of the cemetery in Barrow-in-Furness, to draw up plans for the new resort. Perhaps the choice of planner was prophetic, for although the master plan included space for villas, marine walks, promenades, parades, and the almost obligatory huge Victorian hotel overlooking the sea, the grandiose scheme remained a pipe-dream. Undoubtedly the plan was unveiled at an inopportune moment since the financial and industrial depression of the mid-1870s influenced the fortunes of the new resort and Seascale became a stunted community. In the 20th century,

127 *The hotel and bathing beach, Seascale, about 1850. The Whitehaven and Furness Junction Railway was opened as far as Seascale in 1849.*

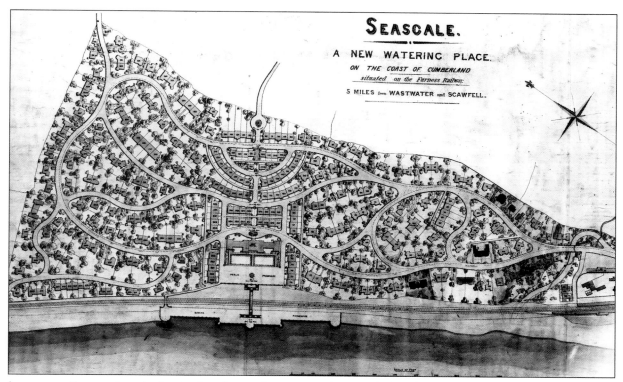

however, the nuclear industry has brought new settlers and the directors of
the Sellafield plant now play golf where the directors of the Furness Railway once envisaged a thriving seaside town.

Silloth, on the Solway coast, also failed to realise the optimistic hopes
expressed for it by its early developers. In 1854 the Carlisle and Silloth Bay
Railway and Dock Company was formed, having as its principal aim the
development of the deep water anchorage of Silloth Bay. Parliamentary
powers were acquired for the development of a dock and a railway connecting the village with Drumburgh on the Port Carlisle Railway and this
line was opened in 1856. For a time, all seemed set fair for the development
of a new town and favourable comparisons were made with the dynamic
growth of West Hartlepool on the east coast. In 1859 the dock was opened
and the town assumed the character of a seaside resort; three graceful
terraces, 'mildly Italianate' according to Sir Nikolaus Pevsner, enhanced
the urban prospect, and a pleasant green separated the town from the
Solway shore and the splendid prospect of the Scottish hills, but the port
failed to compete with the facilities offered by Whitehaven and Workington
and the resort function was merely of local importance. Today, Silloth is
a town which history has passed by, a symbol of the unfulfilled ambitions
of the Victorian planners and speculators and, like Seascale, a community
which did not live up to initial expectations.

128 *Seascale, 'a new
watering place on the
coast of Cumberland'.
The Furness Railway
Company's abortive
designs to convert the
hamlet of Seascale into
a genteel seaside resort,
1870.*

15

Some Nineteenth-Century Rural Industries

Although the 19th century is generally regarded as the age of the steam engine, it is interesting to reflect that, as far as Cumberland and Westmorland were concerned, water power continued to be an important factor in the location of industry in rural areas. In particular, the bobbin industry and the manufacture of gunpowder depended not only on a supply of coppice wood, but also on the availability of fast-flowing streams possessing a head of water. The production of wooden bobbins was necessarily linked to the fortunes of the Lancashire cotton industry and, when that industry experienced the cold wind of economic depression during the 'cotton famine' of the 1860s, the effects were felt in many Cumbrian valleys. In Westmorland there was a marked concentration of the industry in the valley of the River Kent, particularly at Staveley where one company employed over 200 men and apprentices, but not all mills were as large as this; at Rutter Force, near Appleby, the bobbin mill employed a mere 10 hands and there were similar small plants at remote spots such as Howtown on the shores of Ullswater, and on Stainton Beck, near Ravenglass, in West Cumberland. The output from the bobbin mills of North Lancashire and South Westmorland was prodigious and it has been estimated that by the middle of the century about 50 per cent of all the bobbin requirements of the British textile industry came from this area. By the 1870s, however, the industry was in decline; competition from Scandinavia was certainly one factor, but after 1867 the supply of child labour, on which the industry partly depended, was curtailed as a result of the passing of the Factory Act and consequently between 1867 and 1873 several mills closed.

Like the bobbin industry, the manufacture of gunpowder depended on coppiced woodland, which provided the essential charcoal, and water power but, unlike the bobbin mills, the gunpowder works were largely restricted to the valleys of south Westmorland and North Lonsdale. Founded in 1764 when John Wakefield opened his gunpowder mill at Sedgwick, south of Kendal, the industry flourished in an area which had several advantages; not only was there a good supply of silver birch and alder charcoal, but also *savin* charcoal made from the juniper shrub was plentiful, and this made the finest gunpowder. The other necessary raw materials, saltpetre from India and sulphur from Sicily and Italy, could be readily transported from Liverpool to the small port of Milnthorpe, and finally the water power from the co-pious, fast-flowing becks could be harnessed to operate the heavy machinery used in the 'corning' process when the three ingredients were incorporated together. Wakefield's enterprise bore fruit and by the end of the 18th cen-tury two more mills had been opened, one at Bassingill on the River Kent, and the other at Lowwood on the Leven, in North Lonsdale. In 1824 another plant was established, this time at Elterwater, and in 1852 and 1858 two more mills were opened, one at Gatebeck, south of Kendal, and the other at New Sedgwick. Finally, in 1860, the Blackbeck works near Bouth in High Furness began operations. By then the total labour force working in the Lakeland gunpowder mills was probably about 500 men, but after the First World War the demand for 'black powder' declined and production dwin-dled until, in 1937, the last mill, at Gatebeck, closed.

129 *Preparing the pitstead.*

The coppice woods of south Westmorland also supported a wide variety of other industries; the making of charcoal on circular pitsteads had long been an important traditional industry, for 'coles' were not only an impor-tant ingredient of gunpowder, but also the principal smelting agent for the metallurgical industries. Even after the introduction of coke, the famous Backbarrow Furnace on the River Leven in Furness continued to smelt iron in the ancient manner, so stimulating the production of charcoal; indeed, the furnace produced charcoal iron until as late as 1921. Even today the fellsides of scores of Westmorland valleys are dotted with the overgrown pitstead floors where blackened and sweat-streaked 'colliers' once toiled around the clock, poignant reminders of a way of life now gone. Charcoal is still made in Lakeland's woods, but the traditional pitsteads have been replaced by metal kilns and the major market is no longer the

130 *Coaling in pro-gress.*

iron and gunpowder industries but summer barbecues. If 'charcolliers' have declined almost to the point of extinction, the same fate has befallen 'swillers' but there are still one or two of these craftsmen—and one craftswoman—who can weave a spelk or swill basket from thin oak laths. Made with the simplest of tools—a cutting knife, a two-handled shaving knife, and a foot-operated vice known as a 'horse' or a 'mare'— the oval swill baskets found a ready market in those industries requiring a hard-wearing, durable container— coal mining, agriculture, urban refuse collecting, and charcoal burning. In the 19th century thousands of these baskets were sold in Liverpool for the coaling of ships in the days before oil-powered vessels; the average price

131 *A 'swiller's mare', a foot-operated vice, and a partly-finished 'swill' basket made from oak laths.*

132 *A Cumbrian swil-ler. The coppice wood-lands of both Cumber-land and Westmorland provided the oak laths used in the making of these 'spelk' or 'swill' baskets. Here a crafts-man puts the finishing touches to a fine 'swill' at Eskdale Green, Cumberland.*

133 *The black hog of Stricklandgate, Kendal, one of the last reminders of the brush-making industry.*

was one shilling per basket and a good 'swiller' could make just seven in a day. The inevitable march of progress—and with it the advent of polythene—has meant the almost complete demise of this once important craft industry. Other woodland industries have followed suit, and even the manufacture of brushes from the birch, alder, and beech of Westmorland coppices, once localised in Kendal, is now no more, but the beady-eyed, bristly black hog of Stricklandgate still gazes down on the traffic from premises which housed the industry from 1869 until 1922.

Water power was obviously a major factor in the location of industries such as bobbin making, gunpowder, woollen and cotton textiles, papermaking, and even the processing of snuff, and any analysis of these industries clearly shows the importance of the Kent valley. Between 1750 and 1850 there were no fewer than 90 mills in this area, but in the second half of the century this figure fell as steam power made an impact; even then, with typical north-country conservatism, many mill owners were reluctant to abandon their tried and tested water wheels, and therefore the steam engine had less impact here than in other areas. Roy Millward and Adrian Robinson make the surprising but accurate statement that in the early part of the 19th century in the Kent valley there was one mill to every 315 people compared with one mill to every 1,380 in Birmingham at the same time, so on this basis this quiet Westmorland valley seems to have had a more industrialised society than the heartland of the Industrial Revolution. In the second half of the century the pattern changed; steam power became dominant in the Midlands and elsewhere but, in the valley of the Kent,

134 *Cumberland wool —an Eskdale clipping about 1890.*

135 *Spinning wool on the hand-operated spinning wheel at the Hallthwaites Mill, near Millom, south Cumberland, in the early 20th century. The family-owned mill, which specialised in blankets and travelling rugs, finally closed in 1935.*

which lacked local coal resources, industry continued to rely on water power. Above all, water power was cheap and this, together with an abundant supply of local wool, resulted in a resurgence of the ancient Kendal woollen industry; by 1860 almost one third of Kendal's population was employed in the manufacture of woollen goods ranging from cloth and carpets to trousers, horse cloths and, significantly, 'railway rugs' which were much in demand. Elsewhere, too, the industry flourished; at Hallthwaites, nestling at the foot of Black Combe in south-west Cumberland, the woollen mill operated by the Moore family produced blankets, tweed serge, stockings, and hearth rugs, and was typical of many such concerns scattered through the fells of Cumberland and Westmorland. At Millbeck, on the lower slopes of Skiddaw, a whole community depended for its livelihood on the local woollen mills; founded at the end of the 17th century on the site of an ancient fulling mill, the Millbeck complex established for itself an excellent reputation and for a time the mills produced blankets, flannels, kersey and carpets, and markets included such exotic places as New York, New Orleans, Quebec and Montevideo. But competition from the West Riding proved too severe, and in 1886 the mills were closed; the main building is now a private house and a former owner bred goldfish in the millpond which once supplied the power for the mill.

In the same way in which the Kendal woollen industry experienced a revival so, too, the mining and extractive industries underwent a revival in the 19th century. In 1848 the famous Brandlehow Mine near Keswick was re-opened, but with little success until 1852 when a rich vein of lead ore was encountered. However, the difficulties of draining the workings proved

136   The Brandlehow Mine, Derwentwater, 1862. The workings were abandoned in 1864.

insurmountable, and the mine was abandoned in 1864; despite efforts to install a steam engine in the 1880s, the workings were never again profitable. On the other hand, the Greenside lead mine, near Patterdale in Westmorland, proved to be one of the most profitable mines in the area; first opened in the late 18th century, the full potential was not realised until 1825, and 50 years later the mine was producing lead and silver ore worth more than one million pounds sterling. The transport of the ore from this remote valley remained one of the obstacles to development and most of the ore had to be taken by road; before 1824 ore was carried over Sticks Pass to Stoneycroft, in the Newlands valley, where it was smelted, but between 1824 and 1847 the ore was taken by road to Alston for smelting. In 1834 the Greenside company began smelting on the site, but this became uneconomical and after 1867, when the Keswick to Penrith railway line was opened, the dressed ore was taken to Troutbeck station for transport to the smelters of Newcastle. Even in 1911 the mine was producing 3,000 tons of ore per year, but thereafter the output declined and in 1959 the workings were finally closed.

As the momentum of the Industrial Revolution quickened and the rash of red-brick expansion increased, particularly in the growing towns of north-west England, so there developed a demand for roofing slate. Although some of the largest slate quarries in the Lake District were located in the Coniston and Kirkby areas of Furness, there were smaller quarries in such places as Langdale, Troutbeck, and Hartsop, but the most productive workings in the two counties were at Honister. It seems likely that the quarries here were operating in 1643 but the output cannot have been great; however, by 1753 they were in full production. The remoteness of Honister made the shipment of slates somewhat difficult and even in the 19th century strings of pack-horses carried loads of slate by way of the track known as Moses's sled-gate from the quarries on Honister Crag, along the side of Great Gable to Wasdale and on to Drigg on the coast where it was finally loaded onto coasting vessels. It is significant that, despite this incredible journey, it was still considered profitable to transport slate in this way. As the century progressed, the annual output from the quarries increased but, as with the mining of coal and iron, the price of slate was too often underwritten by injury and death. If the actual working of the slate was hazardous, the transporting of it was hair-raising; at Honister and elsewhere, 'trailbarrows' were used to carry the slate down steep fellsides to the nearest road. Simply a heavy wooden sled with shafts or 'stangs', the trailbarrow was loaded with a quarter of a ton of slate every journey and a man took the place of a horse and simply ran down the slope, steering the barrow and being carried forward by the tremendous weight behind him. The wooden sled had then to be carried up the same route for the next trip. This dangerous system of transport continued at Honister until 1881 when a light railway made this operation obsolete.

The opening of the Windermere to Kendal railway line considerably assisted the slate industry in the Langdale area for slate could now be carted to the railhead at Windermere by horse and cart, but no such advantages were available at the isolated Honister quarries; indeed, the workings were so remote that it was customary for quarrymen to live during the week in small huts on the fellside, descending to their homes in Borrowdale and Buttermere only from Saturday night until Monday morning. Ingenuity overcame isolation though, and quarrymen working at Honister communicated with their wives by carrier pigeons. A message could take anything from 10 minutes, the record, to a day, and quite clearly the service depended on the vagaries of the weather, the presence of hawks, and the inclinations of the pigeons but, in the absence of alternatives, the birds proved their worth. In spite of the dangers to life and limb, wages in the quarrying industry were low and hours were long; in the 1830s a good workman received 3s. 6d. per day or £1 1s. 0d. for a six-day week, and for this he was expected to quarry more than a ton of slate each day. Even in the 1870s a 'river' or slate dresser received a mere 3s. 4d. for a working day which began at 7 a.m. and ended at 5.30 p.m., or 4 p.m. on Saturdays.

137 *Sledging slate with a 'trail barrow', Honister. This system of transport was in use until 1881.*

It can be argued that coal mining is not a rural industry, but the importance of this extractive industry to the economy of 19th-century Cumberland assures it of a place in any industrial survey. The improved technology which so characterises the Industrial Revolution meant that mines were better drained and better ventilated, and this in turn meant that shafts could penetrate to greater depths, so increasing output. Although steam power had been employed to drain Stone Pit, Whitehaven, in 1716, it was not until 1789 that a steam engine was used to wind coal to the surface; John Christian Curwen experimented with such an engine at his Workington collieries in that year and was so impressed that two years later eight or nine steam engines were winding coal at Workington. In 1791 a similar engine was installed at Davy Pit, Whitehaven, and this was augmented four years later by another engine at Lady Pit. About the same time a new and improved steam engine, the Heslop engine, made its appearance in West Cumberland and this, too, helped to increase production. New pits were sunk, the most important being the William Pit near Bransty: widely regarded as one of the most advanced collieries in the country, the first coal was raised in 1806 and it remained in production until 1955. The introduction of 'longwall' mining replaced the wasteful 'room and pillar' system in the 1810s, and this made possible the exploitation of previously unworkable seams, Moreover, the expansion of the railway network in the second half of the century gave rise to the development of the coalfield in the Ellen valley and around Aspatria; many of these new pits were small compared with the Whitehaven and Workington collieries and few have left any serious scars on the rural landscape. By 1860 Cumberland coal production had exceeded one million tons a year, but by the end of the century the output was more than two million tons; during the same period employment in mining increased from between 3,000 and 4,000 to more than 8,000 people. As with iron mining, the 20th century brought a reversal of the trends which characterised the West Cumberland coalfield in the 19th; as the richer seams became worked out, the cost of mining increased and pits were closed. Today, no deep-mined coal is produced in Cumberland.

Epilogue

Cumbria—The Land of the Cymry

Like many other upland areas of Britain, the fells and dales of north-west England have traditionally resisted change; indeed, one of the threads running through the pattern of history of both Cumberland and Westmorland has been an innate conservatism and hostility to innovation and new techniques. In part this can be explained by the isolation of the area, the tenacity of Cumbrians and their resilience to new ideas. Yet, for all that, the inevitability of change and the inexorable 'march of progress' has to be acknowledged; stone gave way to bronze which in turn gave way to iron; horse-drawn carriages became horse-less; the heavy, inefficient wooden plough succumbed to the light iron plough which, in turn, has been superseded by the tractor. The coal mines and iron works have been replaced by

138 *Sellafield nuclear plant provides an awesome background for the early Bronze-Age burial circle at Grey Croft, Seascale, Cumberland. The stone circle was partly restored in 1949.*

the nuclear industry and Sellafield, in the 1930s merely the name of a small farmstead near the coast between Seascale and St Bees Head, is now known throughout the world.

For many residents of the former counties of Cumberland and Westmorland, the extinguishing in 1974 of the historic counties and the amalgamation with part of Lancashire and a fragment of the West Riding of Yorkshire was a 'shot-gun marriage' which in some quarters was, and still is, vehemently resisted. Indeed, the town of Appleby insists that its official title is 'Appleby-in-Westmorland' despite the fact that, according to Westminster bureaucrats, the county no longer exists. To others, however, it seemed a logical step for these largely rural communities having the same broad cultural heritage to unite into a new county. The arguments for and against the county of Cumbria and, in particular, the wisdom or otherwise of having Carlisle as its administrative centre, continue to rumble, but in 1995 the Local Government Commissioners decided—against the odds— that the county should remain undivided.

It has been said that Cumbria is more a country than a county and there is a degree of truth in this. Many of the elements which characterise the English landscape are here—the silver-grey limestone uplands, the lonely Solway marshes, the familiar tarns, lakes and mountains of the central fells, the austere Pennine moorlands, the sun-dappled patchwork fields of

139 *Ennerdale Forest, Cumberland. When this plantation was established by the Forestry Commission between 1927 and 1929, some 2,000 Herdwick sheep were displaced from their traditional pasture and the ruler-straight lines and single-species planting evoked considerable hostile criticism. Today, the Forestry Commission takes a far more enlightened view of landscape evolution—but if privatisation continues, will any new owner share the same sympathetic outlook?*

140 *A coach and car park, Bowness, Westmorland. Twenty million people live within a three-hour drive of the Lake District. Are we in danger of turning the Lake District National Park into a National Car Park?*

the Eden valley and West Cumberland, all combine to form one of the most beautiful areas of Britain. But for many people the name Cumbria is synonymous with the Lake District National Park; created in 1951, it then straddled three counties, Cumberland, Westmorland and Lancashire. Today the 880 square miles of the Lake District National Park, together with a part of the Yorkshire Dales National Park, lie within the county of Cumbria. As one of the most popular National Parks in Britain, the Lake District presents the planners with special challenges: can the qualities of peace and quiet, remoteness and wilderness be preserved or are they to be steadily eroded by the millions of visitors who flock to this area in order to enjoy precisely those qualities? Are we in danger of creating a museum or 'theme park' landscape? And how will the thorny question of second homes and selective rural migration influence the social well-being of the area? Can tourist traffic be regulated or will the National Park become a National Car Park? On the answers to these questions depends the character of this unique region.

Cumbria, however, is more than merely the Lake District National Park. The closing of the coal pits and the extinguishing of the iron furnaces has precipitated serious problems in south and west Cumberland and towns like Millom are now seeking a more stable economic future; yet it is too easy to portray these former industrial and mining centres as full of depressed and dispirited people living in run-down terraced houses. Fortunately there is another and more optimistic side of the coin, ably expressed by the late Norman Nicholson:

141 *The Haweswater Reservoir, Westmorland. The construction of the dam in 1929 resulted in the raising of the level of the lake by 95 feet and the consequent destruction of the village of Mardale with its school, the* Dun Bull Inn, *the 17th-century church and four farms. Occasionally, when the 'draw-down' effect is great, the walls and field patterns of the drowned village can once again be distinguished as in the bottom photograph taken in summer, 1984.*

142 *Designed to en-hance the industrial prospects of the Workington-Whitehaven area and to relieve Keswick of the intoler-able summer tourist traffic, the by-pass and the 'improvement' of the old A66 road gave rise to one of the most fiercely contested conser-vationist debates of the 20th century.*

Many men who worked at the iron works and Hodbarrow live, not in dark streets in the shadow of the slagbank, but in new council houses that open straight on to meadows sweeping up to the hills. From their bedroom windows they have views of nearly all the higher peaks of the Lakes, and only a mile away, to the west, are the magnificent sand-dunes of Haverigg and mile after mile of one of the least-spoiled coasts in all England. This is surely the kind of environment that more people are going to demand, in the future, not just for holidays, but for everyday background to their working life.

Technically, Cumberland and Westmorland are no more; Cumbria—'the Land of the Cymry'—has been reborn in the 20th century but, as in the past, man will continue to modify and change the Cumbrian environ-ment. In 1932 Professor W.G. Collingwood wrote the preface to the second edition of *The Lake Counties*; his observations are interesting, even today:

And for my own part let me confess that I never could have believed our Lake Counties had changed so greatly in thirty years, and that under my very eyes. It is like looking at a kaleidoscope. But in such a toy the changes are never for the worse: always into something rich and strange. Can we hope the same for our country? I should like to be one who, as the Romans put it, does not despair of the republic.

It is to be hoped that the future environmental changes will enrich the heritage of Cumbria.

Select Bibliography

The Transactions of the Cumberland and Westmorland Antiquarian and Archaeological Society contain a wealth of material which it is impossible to list here. The papers indicated below have been useful in the compilation of this volume, but students should consult the indices of the Society's Transactions as well as H.W. Hodgson's *Bibliography of the History and Topography of Cumberland and Westmorland* (1968). The titles of books are shown in *italics*, and the titles of articles are placed between inverted commas.

Abbreviations

CW1 Transactions of the Cumberland and Westmorland Antiquarian and Archaeological Society, Old Series, 1866-1900

CW2 Transactions of the Cumberland and Westmorland Antiquarian and Archaeological Society, New Series, 1901-present

Allan, M., *The Roman Route Across the Northern Lake District*, 1994

Armstrong, A.M., Mawer, A., Stenton, F.M., and Dickins, B., *The Place Names of Cumberland*, 3 vols., 1950

Ayton, R. and Daniell, W., *A Voyage Round Great Britain 1813-1823*, reprinted 1978

Bailey, J., and Culley, G., *A General View of the Agriculture of the County of Cumberland*, 1794

Bailey, R.N., *Viking Age Sculpture in Northern England*, 1980

Bainbridge, T.H., 'Eighteenth century agriculture in Cumbria', *CW2*, 44

Barber, R., *Iron Ore and After*, 1976

Barnes, H., 'Visitations of the plague in Cumberland and Westmorland', *CW1*, 11

Bellhouse, R.L., 'Roman sites on the Cumberland Coast', *CW2*, 54, 57 and 64

Berg, K., 'The Gosforth Cross', *Journal of the Warburg and Courtauld Institutes*, 21, 1958

Blake, B., *The Solway Firth*, 1955

Bott, G., *Keswick*, 1994

Bouch, C.M.L., *Prelates and People of the Lake Counties*, 1948

Bouch, C.M.L. and Jones, G.P., *The Lake Counties, 1500-1830*, 1962

Bragg, M., *The Land of the Lakes*, 1983

Breeze, D.J. and Dobson, B., *Hadrian's Wall*, 1978

Brunskill, R.W., *Vernacular Architecture of the Lake Counties*, 1974

Caine, C., *Cleator and Cleator Moor, Past and Present*, 1916

Clare, T., *Archaeological Sites of the Lake District*, 1981

Collier, S., *Whitehaven 1660-1800*, 1991

Collingwood, R.G., *Roman Eskdale*, n.d.

Collingwood, R.G., *A Guide to the Roman Wall*, 5th edn., revised by Sir I.A. Richmond, 1948

Collingwood, W.G., 'The Vikings in Lakeland', *Saga-Book of the Viking Club*, Vol.1, 1892-1896

Collingwood, W.G., *Elizabethan Keswick*, 1912

Collingwood, W.G., *Lake District History*, 1925

Collingwood, W.G., *Northumbrian Crosses of the Pre-Norman Age*, 1927

Curwen, J.F., *Kirkbie-Kendall*, 1900

Curwen, J.F., *The Castles and Fortified Towers of Cumberland, Westmorland and Lancashire, North-of-the-Sands*, 1913

Curwen, J.F., 'The Lancaster Canal', *CW2*, 16-17

Curwen, J.F., 'The Chorography or a Descriptive Catalogue of the Printed Maps of Cumberland and Westmorland', *CW2*, 18

Darbyshire, R.D., 'Notes on the Discoveries in Ehenside Tarn, Cumberland', *Archaeologia*, 44, 1874

Elliott, G., 'The system of cultivation and evidence of enclosure in the Cumberland open fields in the 16th century', *CW2*, 59

Ellwood, T., 'Numerals formerly used for sheepscoring in the Lake counties', *CW1*, 3

Fell, C., *Early Settlement in the Lake Counties*, 1972

Fletcher, H.A., 'The Archaeology of the West Cumberland iron trade', *CW1*, 5

Fletcher, I., 'The Archaeology of the West Cumberland coal trade', *CW1*, 3

Garnett, F.W., *Westmorland Agriculture, 1800-1900*, 1912

Grainger, G. and Collingwood, W.G., *Register and Records of Holm Cultram*, 1929

Harris, A., 'Millom, a Victorian New Town', *CW2*, 66

Harris, A., 'Denton Holme, Carlisle', *CW2*, 67

Harris, A., *Cumberland Iron, the Story of Hodbarrow Mine, 1855-1968*, 1970

Harris, A., 'Colliery Settlements in East Cumberland', *CW2*, 74

Harris, A. and Davis, R.B., 'The Hodbarrow Iron Mine', *CW2*, 68

Hay, D., *Whitehaven, a Short History*, 1966

Hindle, B.P., *Roads and Trackways of the Lake District*, 1984

Holdgate, M.W., *A History of Appleby*, 1956

Holmes, M., *Appleby Castle*, 1974

Hughes, E., *North Country Life of the Eighteenth Century, Vol.2, Cumberland and Westmorland, 1700-1830*, 1965

Hutchinson, W., *A History of the County of Cumberland*, 2 vols., 1794

Jarvis, R.C., 'Cumberland shipping in the eighteenth century', *CW2*, 54

Jones, B.C., 'The Topography of Medieval Carlisle', *CW2*, 76

Jones, G., *A History of the Vikings*, 1973

Kaye, J.W., 'The Millbeck Woollen Industry', *CW2*, 57

Marshall, J.D., *Old Lakeland*, 1971

Marshall, J.D., 'Kendal in the late seventeenth and early eighteenth centuries', *CW2*, 75

Marshall, J.D. and Davies-Shiel, M., *The Industrial Archaeology of the Lake Counties*, 1969 and 1977

Marshall, J.D., and Davies-Shiel, M., *The Lake District at Work*, 1971

Mawson, D.J.W., 'The Canal that never was; the story of the proposed Newcastle-Maryport Canal, 1794-1797', *CW2*, 75

Maxwell, H., *Chronicles of Lanercost, 1272-1346*, 1913

McIntire, W.T., 'The Port of Milnthorpe', *CW2*, 36

Millward, R. and Robinson, A,, *The Lake District*, 1970

Millward, R. and Robinson, A., *Cumbria*, 1972

Monkhouse, F.J., 'Some Features of the Historical Geography of the German Mining Enterprise in Elizabethan Lakeland', *Geography*, 28, 1943

Nicholson, C., *Annals of Kendal*, 1832

Nicholson, N., *Greater Lakeland*, 1969

Nicolson, J. and Burn, R., *The History and Antiquities of the Counties of Westmorland and Cumberland*, 2 vols., 1777

Parker, C.A., *The Gosforth District*, 2nd edn., 1926

Pearsall, W.H. and Pennington, W., *The Lake District*, 1973

Pevsner, N., *Cumberland and Westmorland* (The Buildings of England series), 1967

Postlethwaite, J., *Mines and Mining in the Lake District*, 3rd edn., 1913

Potter, T.W., 'Excavations at Watercrook, 1974, an interim report', *CW2*, 76

Potter, T.W., 'Excavations at Bowness on Solway', *CW2*, 75

Robinson, J., *Guide to the Lakes*, 1819

Robinson, T., *An Essay towards the Natural History of Westmorland and Cumberland*, 1709

Rollinson, W., *A History of Man in the Lake District*, 1967

Rollinson, W., *Life and Tradition in the Lake District*, 1974

Rollinson, W., *Lakeland Walls*, 1975

Rollinson, W. (ed.), *The Lake District: Landscape Heritage*, 1989

Royal Commission on Historical Monuments, England, *Westmorland*, 1936

Salisbury, C.R., 'The Pleistocene Exploitation of Cumbria: A Review', *CW2*, 92

Scott-Hindson, B., *Whitehaven Harbour*, 1994

Shotter, D.C., *Roman North-West England*, 1984

Smailes, A.E., *North England*, 1960

Smith, A.H., *The Place Names of Westmorland*, 2 vols., 1967

Smith, K., *Carlisle*, 1970

Towill, S., *Carlisle*, 1991

Victoria County History of Cumberland, 2 vols., 1901 and 1905

Walton, J.K. and Marshall, J.D., *The Lake Counties from 1830 to the Mid-twentieth Century*, 1981

Waterhouse, J., *The Stone Circles of Cumbria*, 1985

Westall, O.M. (ed.), *Windermere in the Nineteenth Century*, 1976

Wheatley, J.A., *Bonnie Prince Charlie in Cumberland*, 1903

Winchester, A.J.L., *Landscape and Society in Medieval Cumbria*, 1987

Williams, L.A., *Road Transport in Cumbria in the Nineteenth Century*, 1975

Wood, O., 'The Collieries of J.C. Curwen', *CW2*, 71

Wood, O., *West Cumberland Coal, 1600-1982/3*, 1988

Index

141